THE NAVAJO CODE TALKERS

BY GRETCHEN MCBRIDE

Scott Foresman
is an imprint of

PEARSON

Glenview, Illinois • Boston, Massachusetts • Chandler, Arizona
Upper Saddle River, New Jersey

ISBN 13: 978-0-328-51668-1
ISBN 10:   0-328-51668-6

15   16

Their Story

For many years the story of the Code Talkers could not be told. Their extraordinary service to the United States during a time of war remained a secret.

The Code Talkers were a special group of soldiers who served our country during World War II. Until 1968 our government kept the mission of the Code Talkers top secret. The people who served as Code Talkers could not tell anyone—not even their families— about the work they did in the war, but now their story can be told. It begins with the Diné people.

The Diné now live primarily in the southwestern part of the United States. The language of the Diné is somewhat like the languages of other Native American groups living in the northwestern part of the United States and Canada. However, very few people speak these Native American languages.

A Diné man (1904) and woman with child (1930s)

Diné: The People

The name *Diné* means "The People." The Diné are also known as the Navajo, a name given to the nation by outsiders. Some **scholars** believe *Navajo* comes from a Native American language and means "large area of cultivated land." No matter how others refer to them, the Diné maintain a strong sense of their own identity.

The land the Diné have lived on for centuries in what we know today as Colorado, New Mexico, Utah, and Arizona is sacred to them. As settlers moved from the eastern United States to the west in the middle of the nineteenth century, the Diné and other Native American people had to struggle to keep their traditional homelands.

Monument Valley, in Arizona and Utah,
is part of the Diné homeland.

The Diné faced a difficult time in 1864. They were forced by the United States government to walk three hundred miles to Fort Sumner in New Mexico. At Fort Sumner the Diné people were held against their will until 1868. For people who were so attached to a land they believed to be their natural and sacred homeland, this was a terrible hardship.

Finally, in 1868, a treaty was signed that allowed the Diné to return to their land. Because of the bad treatment they received at the hand of the government, many Diné remained distrustful of the United States government for many years. In spite of this, the Diné came to the defense of the United States during World War I and World War II. They fought for the United States and for their own Diné people.

Traditional Ways

Many people or groups of people have traditions that are special to them and make them unique. The Diné are no different. They are a deeply spiritual people, practicing their **ancient** religious traditions along with other religious traditions brought to them by missionaries.

Just as the land they call their home is special and sacred to them, so are the **ceremonies** that the Diné practice. These ceremonies make up their culture and are a way of life for them. The sacred ceremonies of the Diné teach them about their history, about human responsibilities, or about the world around them. Ceremonies also are used to bless a new home, care for the sick, or bring goodwill to the community.

Some ceremonies involve drypainting, which is made with grains of colored sand. The images created are often symbols of strength for Diné people in need. The drypainting is swept away to end the ceremony.

The Blessing Way is an ancient and sacred ceremony of the Diné. During this ceremony, the people may sing special songs, have a ritual bath, and say prayers. The ceremony is meant to protect the people at a time of change and challenges. The Blessing Way would be important for many of the Diné Code Talkers upon entering World War II.

A Diné creates a drypainting on the floor (top). A close-up of a drypainting shows color and delicate details (bottom).

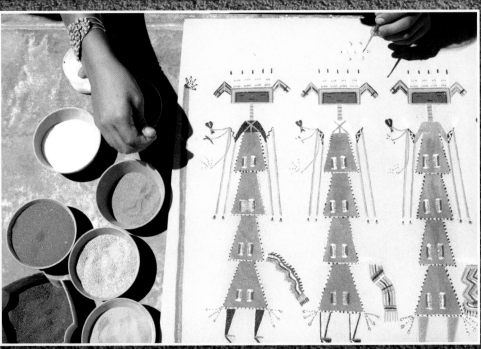

World War II

When the United States entered World War II in 1941, many Diné men enlisted in the armed services. Diné women also volunteered and became part of the Women's Army Corps. For many of these men and women, it would be the first time they would leave the Diné **reservation.** Although life in the military was strange to them, the Diné soldiers excelled in tests of physical endurance. An outdoor life in a harsh environment had prepared them well for this new challenge.

By the end of the war, thirty-six hundred Diné would serve in the armed forces. Of these, more than four hundred would come to be called Code Talkers. They would perform an extraordinary service for their country and their people.

U.S. Marine Code Talkers relay a message with a field radio.

Japan used secret codes before attacking Pearl Harbor.

One of the challenges in any war is communication. Military headquarters must be able to get messages to the soldiers fighting in the field, and the soldiers must be able to report back to headquarters. If an army is to be successful, it is crucial that these communications be kept secret from the other side.

During World War I, the United States set up its first office especially for **cryptography,** the art or process of creating or figuring out secret codes. Even when the nation was not officially at war, this office worked to break the secret codes being used by foreign nations. They were usually successful, but on December 4, 1941, the code that the Japanese had been using suddenly changed. The United States code readers could no longer **decipher** it. This may be one reason the United States Navy was not ready for the attack by the Japanese on Pearl Harbor on December 7, 1941. Clearly, cryptography would be vitally important in World War II.

The Language of the Diné

World War I veteran Philip Johnston knew that being able to send secret messages in an unbreakable code would be important for the United States to win World War II. He also knew that American Indian languages had been used with some success for communications during World War I.

Johnston was the son of missionary parents. While Johnston was growing up, his family lived on a Diné reservation. From the age of four, he had played with the Diné children and had learned to speak their language. The Diné language became almost as familiar to him as the English he spoke with his parents.

As an adult, Philip Johnston realized that the Diné language he had learned as a child was a complicated one, and that not many people outside of the Diné community could speak the language or even understand it when they heard it.

This earthen hogan can be found on a Diné reservation.

Window Rock, in Arizona, is a landmark of the Diné.

Diné is an oral language without a system of writing. Scholars from outside the Diné community who wanted to learn the language tried to write it down the way they heard it, but this was very difficult.

The language of the Diné is not like any of the European languages. The sounds are very different. People who have not grown up speaking it find it difficult to hear the difference between some of the sounds. Like Chinese, Diné is a **tonal** language. This means that making a sound higher or lower in pitch can give the sound a different meaning. The grammar of Diné is also complicated and different from English and other European languages.

Philip Johnston knew that he was one of the few people outside the Diné nation who could speak Diné well. And even he, who had learned the language as a child, could not speak or understand it perfectly. For these reasons, he thought that the Diné language might be a good basis for a secret code.

The Experiment

Philip Johnston thought his idea for a secret code might help his country. Johnston traveled to Camp Elliot in San Diego, where he met with Colonel James E. Jones, the Signal Corps' communications officer for the U.S. Marines. Colonel Jones listened to Johnston speak the Diné language, and he was amazed. He had never heard anything like the sounds Johnston made. Colonel Jones agreed to set up a test of Johnston's idea.

On February 28, 1942, Johnston brought with him to Camp Elliot four Diné who **fluently** spoke both their native language and English. One pair of Diné was given a military message in English. They **translated** the message into Diné and transmitted it by radio to the other pair of Diné in another room. The second pair translated the message back into English. Their work was quick and accurate.

The Marines were impressed and gave Johnston permission to **recruit** Diné men who could speak both Diné and English for the project. The recruits would also have to meet the strict physical requirements for the Marines, and they could be told only that they were to be "specialists." These Diné would come to be known as Code Talkers.

Diné veterans march in a parade.

The Code

It would not be enough to speak Diné over the radio in the field. There were other Diné serving in the military who would understand the language. The military could not risk having those men captured and forced to translate messages.

The Code Talkers first developed a twenty-six-letter alphabet with whole Diné words standing for letters. They would use this to "spell" over the radio. But the vocabulary of the Diné language did not have the words for the military terms that would be used over and over again. For a term such as "tank," the Code Talkers thought of something that reminded them of a tank. They thought of the word "turtle." Other words had some connection to what they stood for; for example, "potato" stood for hand grenade because of the objects' similar shapes.

The Code Talkers started with a simple twenty-six-letter alphabet, but they expanded it to more than four hundred letters to make the code harder to break. If the same word stood for the same letter in every message, an expert could break the code by noticing which words occurred most often in the code. In English, for instance, the letter *e* is the most frequently used letter. It would be easy to figure out which symbol stood for *e*, in a code that used only one symbol for it.

LO-TSO is the Diné word for *battleship.*

Code Talkers' Dictionary

English Term	Diné Word	Literal Translation
America	NE-HE-MAH	our mother
dive bomber	GINI	chicken hawk
fighter plane	DA-HE-TIH-HI	hummingbird
battleship	LO-TSO	whale
destroyer	CA-LO	shark
amphibious	CHAL	frog
anti	WOL-LA-CHEE-TSIN	ant ice
bomb	A-YE-SHI	eggs
bulldozer	DOLA-ALTH-WHOSH	bull sleep
creek	TOH-NIL-TSANH	very little water
farm	MAI-BE-HE-AHGAN	fox arm
not	NI-DAH-THAN-ZIE	no turkey
river	TOH-YIL-KAL	much water

Code Talkers in Battle

The Code Talkers had to memorize the expanded alphabet and long list of code words. They tried to choose code words that would be easy for them to remember. Nothing could be written down in the field, and their transmissions had to be fast and accurate. The lives of American soldiers depended on them.

Philip Johnston's idea proved to be a good one. The Marines continued to recruit Diné who met the requirements for the special program. Code Talkers went through the rigors of basic training with the other recruits and were required to meet strict English and Diné language standards as well. Johnston, although too old to fight in World War II, rejoined the military and trained Code Talkers.

The first Code Talkers reported for combat duty to General Alexander Vandegrift's First Marine Division on Guadalcanal in August 1942. With bravery and skill, the Code Talkers played a part in every important battle in the Pacific. By speaking their secretly coded language over radio, they transmitted crucial battlefield information. Their commitment to their job and their diligent work helped America greatly.

U.S. Marine Code Talkers Corporal Henry Bahe, Jr., and Private First Class George H. Kirk in the jungles of New Guinea, December 1943

U.S. Navy Corsair

The Code Talkers were important to many of the operations of the American military in the Pacific, but perhaps the most important battle was the battle of Iwo Jima. During the battle of Iwo Jima, the Code Talkers worked nonstop sending and receiving hundreds of messages. Their work was flawless.

The tiny island of Iwo Jima, barren and lacking drinkable water, was held firmly by the Japanese. The United States wanted the island because of its strategic location. It would serve as a landing strip for disabled planes as they traveled between aircraft carriers and major Japanese cities. It took an entire month to secure the island, and the cost in lives—both American and Japanese—was tragically high. Almost twenty thousand Americans were wounded, and more than sixty-eight hundred were killed. Almost all of the Japanese soldiers on the island died. The American victory, though costly, would prove to be crucial in winning the war.

American Marines raise the U.S. flag over the Pacific island of Iwo Jima.

Replica of the Congressional Gold
Medal awarded to the Code Talkers

Returning Home

As many as 420 Diné served as Code Talkers during
World War II. These heroes had served their country
in an important way, but there could be no special
recognition for them when they returned home. The
Code Talkers were sworn to secrecy. They could tell
no one of the special code they had created, and they
upheld their vow of secrecy. The code was such a
success in communicating wartime information that it
was kept secret for years after the end of World War II.

Like the other returning Diné soldiers, the Code
Talkers were honored by their community. Their
families performed traditional cleansing ceremonies
to help them recover from their experiences in battle.
Many veterans would become leaders of their people.

Finally, after the order for secrecy was lifted, the
Code Talkers could receive the official honors of their
country. In 1982 President Reagan honored them by
declaring August 14 to be National Code Talkers Day.
In July 2001 President George W. Bush bestowed
the Congressional Gold Medal on the twenty-nine
original Code Talkers. The other Code Talkers received
the Congressional Silver Medal of Honor. The code
created by the Code Talkers remains the only code
never to be broken by an opponent.

A Diné Code Talker receives the Congressional Gold Medal from President George W. Bush in 2001.

Now Try This

SEND CODED MESSAGES

See if you could be a cryptographer! The Code Talkers used a spoken code and used entire Diné words to stand for single letters. Let's see if you can make up a written code using just a letter, number, or symbol for each letter.

A	B	C	D	E	F	G	H	I	J	K	L	M	N	O
1	Z	Y	X	2	J	V	T	3	B	S	P	W	4	C

Create your own code using letters and numbers.

X 2 Y C X 2

D E C O D E

Try to break the codes of another team.

22

1. With a partner, write down our twenty-six-letter alphabet and decide on a symbol—it could be another letter or a number—to stand for each letter.

2. Now, you and your partner can decide what kinds of messages you are likely to send each other. Perhaps you would like to talk about your favorite after-school activities. Come up with a list of words that you are likely to need for your messages. Now decide on the list of code words to use instead. For instance, perhaps your code word for "basketball" could be "sun." (A basketball is round like the Sun.) The alphabet and code word lists will be the two keys you use for decoding messages.

3. Write a four-line message to your partner. If any words in your message have code words, use the code words. Next, use your alphabet list to change your message into code. Then exchange messages with your partner. Using your decoding keys, see how quickly and accurately you can decode your partner's message.

4. Exchange your keys with another team, and see if you can write and decode messages in their secret code.

5. Here is the biggest challenge: Exchange messages with another team without exchanging the code word keys. Can you break their code?

Glossary

ancient *adj.* very old or of times long past.

ceremonies *n.* formal acts or sets of acts performed according to tradition for a special purpose.

cryptography *n.* the art or process of creating or figuring out secret codes.

decipher *v.* to make out the meaning of something that is puzzling or not clear.

fluently *adv.* smoothly; easily.

recruit *v.* to sign up persons, especially for military service.

reservation *n.* land set aside by the government for a special use, especially for the use of a Native American nation.

scholars *n.* people who have much knowledge.

tonal *adj.* of or relating to the high or low pitch of a sound.

translated *v.* changed from one language into another.

WELLNESS FOR WINNERS

Your Guide to Wellness, Success, and Happiness

created by

Sherri Leopold and Evan Trad

Action Takers Publishing™
San Diego, California

Action Takers Publishing™
www.actiontakerspublishing.com

ebook ISBN: 978-1-956665-01-7
Paperback ISBN: 978-1-956665-02-4

Cover Design by Sam Art Studio
Printed in the United States of America

TABLE OF CONTENTS

Be brave and share your weaknesses, for in your weaknesses others see your strengths.

~Lynda Sunshine West

A WINNING NOTE FROM SHERRI LEOPOLD AND EVAN TRAD

Wellness: the quality or state of being in good health especially as an actively sought goal

Together we are well. Together we win!

This is a page in the story of Sherri Leopold and Evan Trad.

From meeting randomly on a plane to developing a lifelong friendship, we have laughed, cried, worried, celebrated, and traveled together. We have genuinely grown together. In fact, we have our own hashtag- #adventureswithsherriandevan. This book is one of our adventures.

During one of our long conversations about life, health, and business, Evan suggested we move forward with the book idea we had tossed about.

Evan was the action taker that put the project/goal in motion. This book came to fruition almost one year to the day that we made that decision.

Many steps along the way were rocky and had several detours. We remained true to our one purpose... helping people win through wellness.

We wanted to create a book that would highlight stories of those who had succeeded on the wellness journey, whether it was mental, emotional, physical, or spiritual health (MEPS). We have always used our own stories to empower others in their health and wellness journeys. We knew we wouldn't have to look far to find other incredible people who would inspire you, give you hope, and help you believe and understand the best is yet to be!

One by one these authors have poured themselves into their stories to inspire and enlighten you. Our most sincere desire is for hope to bloom after reading these winners stories. May that hope lead to courage, and that courage lead to action.

Each story is sprinkled with the actions necessary to become wellness winners.

It's your turn.

It's your time.

Take Action.

Choose to be Well. Choose to Win!

Sherri Leopold and Evan Trad

A SPECIAL NOTE ABOUT THE CHARITY

100% of the net proceeds of the sales of this book will be donated to Girls on the Run, a 501(c)(3) nonprofit charity whose mission is to reach girls at a critical stage, strengthening their confidence at a time when society begins to tell them they can't. Underscoring the important connection between physical and emotional health, Girls on the Run's program addresses the whole girl when she needs it the most.

For further information or to make a donation, visit their website at www.girlsontherun.org.

CHAPTER ONE

CHANGE YOUR CHOICES...
AND YOUR CHOICES CHANGE!

by Sherri Leopold
CEO and Founder, Dream Big with Sherri Leopold
https://sherrileopold.com

O h no, not again! Slam goes the door. Lots of yelling, and now my mom is crying. She is trying to reason with him. I am scared, hiding under the covers in my room and crying. I can't stay here by myself. I run out the door and across the hall and crawl into one of my older brothers' bed. At eight years old, he is three years older than me. We just huddled together until the yelling and crying stopped. This seems like a lifetime ago; as it's been more than 50 years.

Until recently, I had no idea why I felt so consumed with helping people Stand UP and Stand OUT. That's my tag line for my business Dream BIG with Sherri Leopold. I primarily focus on women. I watched my mother, who I believed was so strong, still struggle with feeling worthy. Even though I have always felt compelled to help the underdog and be the cheerleader for those who weren't able to cheer for themselves, I didn't realize until 54 years old why this is so critically important to me. Personally, I am strong, and perhaps border on defiant at times. The urge to fight is fierce. A more accurate way to state this is, I will not be kept down. I will not be silenced. Maybe it was those three older brothers who taught me to be tough, or maybe it was growing up in such chaos and resolving to NEVER find myself in that position. Either way, it has shaped the woman I am today.

I have spent quite a bit of time thinking about what must have been going through my mother's head. At that time, she worked in the restaurant sector as a hostess, manager, and waitress. She always excelled and was an incredibly hard worker. I'd like to think much of my work ethic came from watching her. She always served others. It always perplexed me that she seemed to serve everyone else and not herself. Perhaps it was just me that was confused. I don't know why, but she always seemed to put everyone before her. I do understand wanting to be helpful to other people, but sacrificing yourself didn't seem right.

My mother was always the fixer. I, too, love being a fixer. We are very similar in many ways. They say, "The apple doesn't fall far from the tree," and that's definitely me. This has created in me a very determined need to stand up for myself. I am not sure if having such an incredible father in my life is why I knew there was something better, but my life did change when I turned twelve. By this time, I had a sister who was five years old and I felt a bit lost. I felt as if I didn't have any voice at all. My sister, who is my stepfather's daughter, was impacted and suffered through those abusive episodes as well. The difference between us was that the abusive man wasn't really my dad. That was her father and that was a lot for her to deal with.

I would like to point out that my stepfather is not a horrible man. He is actually a phenomenal person; he would give the shirt off his back to you or do anything he could to help, when he wasn't drinking. It was a literal Dr. Jekyll/Mr. Hyde scenario. I loved him and hated him at the same time. Reflecting back, I suppose that was one of the things that was difficult for my mother as well. He was very loving, kind, and decent when sober. Add alcohol, and the world tilted a bit on its axis.

As a child, I can't quite express how confusing this felt. I did not understand how someone could be so kind one day, and the next day be someone completely different. This also shaped who I am today. I am known to say that no matter where you meet me, or how you meet me, you will always get the real me. I have no facáde. I am completely and wholly me at all times.

At twelve years old, when I realized I could make a different choice using my voice, I did not realize there were legal implications that would have prevented me from actually moving with my father and stepmother before that age. At twelve, however, I was considered old enough to decide where I wanted to live and with whom. I must have been sharing about a recent episode of abusive drunken behavior, and my father said innocently, "You know you don't have to stay, right?" The truth was, I did NOT understand that. That one conversation changed my life. That precise moment when I said, "Yes, I want to come and live with you," was both exciting and depressing at the same time. I felt like I was saving myself, but abandoning my sister to a terrible situation.

I did not have the courage to tell my mother; my father offered to tell her. She did not argue, but I know she was devastated. She knew why I was leaving, but it didn't soothe the wound. I still saw her and my step-father and sister, but it was far less.

I spent much of the next two years learning a different family structure. I learned that people ate dinner at specific times. I learned there were better ways of communicating than what I had experienced. I learned that laundry could be done routinely and that vegetables were common at every dinner meal. I stopped eating bread with just garlic salt on it or bread with butter caked with sugar for a meal. I think I might have felt a bit like Dorothy when she stepped out of her house after the tornado. The entire world seemed different to me.

I began to participate in school activities and join in sports, etc. I never had a ride to or from school before I moved. Perhaps I could have figured it out had I found a way to use my voice before that. You don't know what you don't know.

Living with my father, I began to go to bed at a regular time. That may seem to many like a routine thing. For me, however, I would always want to wait until my mom returned home from waitressing, which was usually 10:30 to 11:00 at night. I shudder to think how this affected my brain development. Because my mom missed so much time with us, it was hard for her to say no to us staying up like that. This did not help my school performance, I am sure. I was definitely not used to having two parents at home every night, but I realized I liked it.

This became part of my process of understanding that if I wanted something, I needed to speak up. I began to express to my dad and stepmother when I needed things such as clothes, permission slips signed, and things of that nature. At mom's house, I was always the one who was missing the permission slip or dressed in mismatched clothes. This is likely why I am always supporting the person who feels a bit lost, left out, or the one who doesn't feel like they fit in. I always want to champion those who don't feel strong. I know what it was like to feel weak, to be the one who felt like they didn't belong, or wasn't worthy.

This brings me to why I am so passionate about helping others Stand UP and Stand OUT as the unrepeatable miracle that they are. Regardless of our circumstances, we are still unique exactly as we are. There is no one else who thinks like we do. There is no one else who will have the same experiences the exact same way that we do. Each of us has a story that can impact others. I understand that my story of living in a home with domestic violence is a difficult one to hear and live through, but is necessary to be talked about.

Without darkness, there is no light.

I will continue to share, even though it is difficult to talk about. I am solution oriented, which is a gift from my mother. She could take any situation and figure it out. Just like what Marie Forleo's mother taught Marie, my mother taught me, "Everything is figureoutable!" I agree. Because we are an unrepeatable miracle, meaning we are not duplicated in any way on this planet, we have strengths that no one has. Some people need help in understanding their talents, strengths, and gifts. Know those strengths; and you can share them.

My mission is to help people (women especially) understand themselves and their strengths so well that, at any given time, they can articulate what makes them unique. When you know what your personal strengths are, you are able to Stand UP and Stand OUT as the unique human you are. I know what my gifts and strengths are, and I use those talents to change the world, one ... person ... at ... a ... time. I am a mirror to others to see their inner beauty and true greatness.

I am known for saying, "Choices create change. Change your choices, and your choices change." This is the story of my life. When I found my voice at age twelve, I used it to make a choice to go live with my father. In doing so, my choices changed. Those choices created opportunities that turned into lifelong friendships, better health, and the ability to believe in myself.

People often say that they have no choice. I wholeheartedly disagree. I believe we have unlimited choices. Sometimes our choices all seem crappy. This causes us to feel we don't have a choice. We do have a choice, it's just not one we want to make! The phenomenal reality about choices is you never have just one. When you make one, you will have more immediately! Life is 100% comprised of the billions of choices we are privileged make. I wasn't stuck. I had choices. Even if I wasn't aware of it, I still had them. When I realized I could make some different choices, I made them. They were very hard choices. There were very uncomfortable emotions attached to my decisions and choices. Not just for myself, but for those around me.

When I think back to that 5-year-old cowering under the covers with my brother, I think about my mother and how she didn't feel capable of standing up for herself. As a parent myself, I realize that the therapist I went to in college was right. It wasn't something the therapist said; it's what she helped me understand, that my mother was doing the best she could, with what she had, at the time. She made her choices and lived with the results.

Because I found my voice at twelve, I realized that I was in charge of ME. As an adult, I knew I had many choices. My voice could (and would) mandate my choice!

That is an incredibly powerful concept when you realize that you have the power to create your life. I could have chosen a life of chaos, but I didn't. I am so grateful for the experiences I have had, both good and challenging. Each experience we have creates the unique human that we are. Standing UP and Standing OUT is a choice. Being YOU is always going to be your best choice! Like when Dorothy clicked her heels and said, "There's no place like home"!

Home = YOU, the one and only.

The way to have true success, happiness, and wellness, is to be the unique one-of-a-kind, unrepeatable miracle that is YOU!

Choose YOU first! (Your choices will expand exponentially.)

SHERRI LEOPOLD

Sherri Leopold is a Mentor, 6 times International Bestselling Author, Speaker, Founder and CEO of Dream Big with Sherri Leopold. She released her first book in June of 2019 called *Self-Bullying: What to Do When the Bully Is YOU!* As Leader of the Stop Self-Bullying Movement, Sherri released her program called W.O.W. (War On Words) Warriors. The Stop Self- Bullying Program teaches self-love and acceptance by teaching you to Stand UP and Stand OUT as the unrepeatable miracle you are. Sherri is a television host of the show Outside the Box with Sherri Leopold on Legrity Media TV and has worked in the Network Marketing/Direct Selling industry for 24 years, sharing her expertise in speaking, mentoring, and team building. She is an Independent 200K Brand Promoter, and autobonus earner and 20-time trip earner for Thrive by Le-Vel. Sherri is also a Dr. Amen Licensed Brain Trainer. She is passionate about teaching about brain health and improving memory. She excels in the health and wellness industry by combining the physical and the emotional to support complete transformation. Life is meant to be lived fully!

You can connect with Sherri here: https://sherrileopold.com.

CHAPTER TWO

MENTAL TOUGHNESS: IT'S WORTH FIGHTING FOR

by Evan Trad
CEO & Visionary, TEAM Evan
www.goteamevan.com

From a young age, I was a fighter. My earliest memory at four years old was being carried down a long hospital hallway decorated with colorful paintings. I cried so hard, tears streamed down my face. The nurse carrying me was trying to calm me by pointing to the colorful paintings as we walked toward the operating room. This was not the first time I was heading to the operating room, but this time was different because this time I could remember I was aware of what was happening. My body continued to tremble as the nurse continued to work to calm my nerves. I was born with many health challenges, including having one kidney and heart problems. Most of these could have led to my early death but, as I said, I am a fighter. I persevered through them all to grow into the healthy, confident, and mentally tough man that I am today! I shifted my mindset to become mentally tough. Even with a fighting spirit, I needed a plan. With these specific five mindset practices, I manage and overcome any challenging situations that life throws my direction. As a teacher, I am passionate about helping others learn. I believe I can help you become mentally tough, too.

I define being mentally tough as the ability to resist, manage, and overcome doubts, worries, concerns, and circumstances that prevent you from succeeding. This is not innate in every person. However, it can be learned! There are five practices that can build mental toughness when practiced regularly: 1) learning from your mistakes, 2) reflection, 3) staying positive, 4) building confidence, and 5) never giving up! These are powerful practices that when focused on regularly will build you into a mentally tough warrior!

Learn From Your Mistakes

As a kid, the idea of getting in trouble produced panic-like symptoms in my body. Such as a racing heart, body sweats, stomach in a knot, and breathing heavily. I would do anything I could to avoid getting in trouble. This included telling lies.

Since the idea of getting in trouble was so stressful, I believed I could avoid all the panic symptoms in my body if I just lied. If I did something wrong or made a mistake, but could hide it–problem solved. Sometimes these would be little white lies, but other times it would turn into a thick web of lies, upon lies, and I couldn't keep track. At times, I wouldn't know what was true or even why I told the lies in the first place. That was also stressful. I am an only child and this created the problem that there wasn't anyone else to blame. Whenever I did something wrong at home and I tried to lie in an attempt to avoid punishment, it only led to bigger problems. My mom knew there could be no one else who caused the problem! It was a vicious circle and none of it avoided the stress, it just postponed it. This only led to bigger punishments and larger problems like lacking self-confidence.

As I grew older and matured, I realized that telling lies to avoid problems and punishment made things worse. In the end, being truthful upfront led to more calm for me and quicker resolutions. I also realized that my efforts to avoid punishment didn't allow me to learn from my mistakes but instead kept me repeating the same mistakes over and over. When I learned the importance of being truthful, accepting my mistake, reflecting on what happened, life became much easier. Ironically, I actually got into far less trouble and made fewer mistakes. This magically alleviated all the body stressors I had inadvertently created.

Reflection

As I have grown, I have realized the power that reflection has had on everything I do in my life. From my career, relationships, friendships, and everything in between, reflection has been an integral part of the process. The power of reflection has allowed me to grow as a person, reach my goals, and grow professionally. I am building and creating beautiful parts of my life I never thought possible.

I have not always been as reflective as I could have been. I moved through my life without much thought. I made decisions without much forethought. This cost me growth in many areas of my life. At the time, I had no idea because I was not reflecting on aspects of my life that were important to me or my personal growth. Can you expect to move forward or make changes if you are not thinking about where you have been and where you want to go? For me, that answer was no. Reflection is essential to making changes in your life.

I came to understand the importance of reflection after having read a book that stresses the importance of journaling for ten minutes each morning. Hal Elrod and The Miracle Morning helped me understand this concept. I began the practice and realized how empowering and eye-opening it was to spend ten minutes reflecting on whatever came to my mind that morning. This journaling practice led me to create changes in my life including making new friends, finding mentors, making significant career moves, and more.

As I have practiced daily reflection, it has taken many different shapes and forms over time. I use the time to continue to journal, meditate, share gratitude, but also to evaluate and think deeply about things that might be holding me back or making me feel unsettled. The time I take to reflect has grown, too. I have become comfortable with silence. I enjoy the silence now and allow myself time to get lost in thought. Letting the power of reflection just take over. Reflection allows you to learn to be with yourself and love it.

Stay Positive

Since the age of ten, I have wanted to be a teacher. As I prepared to leave for college, I was excited to begin my journey and fulfill this dream. My dream did not go according to plan. My dream was almost crushed at the end of my first year when I met with my academic advisor. Upon looking at my grades, he simply said I needed to find a new major.

To say I felt defeated at that moment was an understatement. What was I going to do? Was there another option? What other career could I do or want to do? I had these and a million questions whirling around in my head. I felt myself losing my long-held dream.

As I sauntered back to my residence hall, my mind spinning and tears welling in the corners of my eyes, I was faced with a choice: give up and let your dream die or find another way. Being born the fighter I am, I took a deep breath, said to myself: there must be another way! I spent that night scouring the university catalog for a new major. I found that there was a degree in special education and I met the requirements. The next day, I changed my major. I graduated as a special education teacher and fulfilled the dream of becoming a teacher.

When I had overwhelming feelings of sadness and defeat, I could have let the negative thoughts take over. I shifted my thinking by taking a pause, took a deep breath, and gave myself a choice. I had the option to give up and let the dream die or find another way. This pause and giving myself a choice allowed me to reset my thinking. I chose a positive mindset. We always have a choice.

Build Confidence

I have not always been confident. In fact, if you were to ask me three years ago if I would be a published author or speaking to crowds I would have laughed in your face. In fact, for most of my life, I didn't mind being a follower. Yes, I had a lot of qualities of a great leader, but I also had that little mickey mouse voice in the back of my head saying those defeating statements that I began to believe might be true.

My confidence in myself began to build when I began to follow a strict morning routine. This routine included physical activity, I AM statements, journaling gratitude/reflections, and taking a high-quality supplement. Changing these aspects of my morning routine helped elevate my self-confidence.

Each morning I would move my body in some form. I started with yoga because it allowed me to build my physical movement and reflect at the same time. Yoga turned into strength training and cycling. The more I moved my body, the faster I saw changes and the more confidence I felt.

I began to also say I AM statements to myself. Some feel they are trendy, I say they are powerful. I would align these statements with who I was becoming as a person, or to goals I wanted to achieve. I would repeat them to myself ten times. "I am confident," "I am kind," "I am a public speaker," "I am a published author," etc. You are reading one of my I AMs.

Each day, I'd write ten items I was grateful for. The list changed daily but there would be constants (i.e., family, house, career, etc.). The gratitudes remind me of how hard I have worked and the accomplishments support my self-confidence.

Never Give Up

I always loved school. It came easy to me, except for math. I struggled in math. I practiced math facts for endless hours. Watching as the pile of flashcards on the table in the "wrong" pile grows. The tight knot in your stomach and feeling like you will never learn them and hearing your teacher's reminder that practice makes perfect. Back to the table with the mounting pile of flashcards. Wrong. Wrong again. Defeated. Confused. Why was math so difficult for me?

Math continued to be a struggle. The fighter in me knew I could master it. I needed to think about it differently. I wouldn't give up. I wanted to, but I knew I couldn't. I was afraid my brain couldn't work correctly to excel at math, but I kept at it. I worked to learn in some creative ways. The beauty of math, as with many of life's challenges, is there are many ways to get to the solution. This flexibility allowed me to think differently and become good at what was my biggest challenge.

My own struggles and perseverance have allowed me to have empathy towards students in my classroom who are showing similar struggles. I share my personal story with them. I teach them creative solutions and encourage that drive to NEVER give up. I teach them to problem solve in a different way such as thinking creatively, finding a new strategy, asking for help to handle the struggle. When my students overcome the challenge, we all get to feel that pride and accomplishment together. They begin to understand the power of never giving up, just as I have.

Life isn't easy and having mental toughness isn't easy either. The skills needed to be mentally tough aren't easy to acquire and require practice. It takes determination to learn and practice them daily. When you are able to master them, you are able to manage anything that life serves you up. By being mentally tough, you are able to navigate any situation and turn it into the outcome that you desire.

From a young age, I was a fighter that continued to be a warrior with my mental toughness! As life got hard, I continued to stand up and show I was not able to be knocked down. Each and every day I work to become more mentally tough. These 5 practices: learning from past mistakes, reflecting, staying positive, building my confidence, and never giving up have served me well! May these 5 practices lead you to be mentally tough!

EVAN TRAD

Evan Trad is a distinguished educator and entrepreneur from Chicago, Illinois. Evan's entrepreneur journey began through network marketing where he learned his business management skills. In learning to manage and grow his own business, he realized his passion--empowering people with disabilities.

Evan is passionate about helping people with disabilities succeed in school and in life. Evan was the founding special educator at a new charter school in Chicago, where, for nearly ten years, he built the special education program from the ground floor and is and continues to thrive today. Evan now works to build a successful inclusion special education program at a high performing public school in Chicago.

Evan's passion for empowering kids with disabilities and his own entrepreneurial spirit fused together in 2019 when he founded his business Team EVAN. He has the vision that people with disabilities have potential and are more than their disability. Team EVAN passionately develops people with disabilities to more than and stronger than their limitations, shaping their vision into reality, to become successful entrepreneurs.

This passion spilled over into the world of theater where he serves as president of the board of directors for Tellin' Tales Theatre company, whose mission is to shatter barriers between the disabled and non-disabled worlds. A mission that holds true to Evan's philosophy of empowering others to live the life they deserve.

You can connect with Evan here: www.goteamevan.com.

CHAPTER THREE

DO IT BECAUSE YOU'RE SCARED

by Lynda Sunshine West
Founder & CEO, Action Takers Publishing™
www.ActionTakersPublishing.com

Before diving into this chapter, I did a little bit of research. What exactly do the words "Wellness" and "Winners" mean?

According to Merriam-Webster's Dictionary, the word "Wellness" is defined as 'the quality or state of being in good health especially as an actively sought goal lifestyle that promotes wellness' and "Winners" is defined as 'one that wins: such as one that is successful especially through praiseworthy ability and hard work.'

Okay. Now that I have that out of the way, I can get started.

At this time of my life, age 58, I am actually in the worst physical shape I've ever been in my entire life. So, when this book title came up, I started doubting myself and thinking that I have no value to offer to this book. Then it hit me. Wellness is not only in physical health, but is also in mental health. While I am physically in the worst shape I've ever been, I am in the absolute best shape I've ever been in mentally.

As we get older, things shift in our bodies. We can either succumb to the shifts or we can make changes in our lives so that we don't falter. I am in a place in my life where my mental capacity means more to me than my physical capacity. It's weird, though, because I was never into my physical shape much, even though I was a bodybuilder when I was younger. As I look back on my life, I realize that my being in shape as a bodybuilder was more something that I did because I wanted the man I loved to love me back.

I did many things in my life, for love.

I let love guide me because I never felt loved as a child and never loved myself until I started my personal development journey at age 51. I like to say that I'm seven years old because I'm still learning a lot about what love means to me and what it means to be loved.

I grew up in a very volatile, abusive alcoholic household and, unfortunately, my first marriage was to someone just like my dad. While my dad's abuse was physical and verbal, my ex-husband's abuse of choice was verbal. It was quite damaging.

There's a nursery rhyme that says, "Sticks and stones may break my bones, but words will never hurt me." I beg to differ. Words can adversely affect your life, if you let them. I spent the first few years of my life allowing the verbal abuse that I experienced to adversely affect me. Those words caused so much pain and anguish and anxiety and fear and,… you name it.

Daily for two years being called 'stupid' and 'ignorant' were probably the two most damaging words I experienced in my entire life. The worst part is that I believed him. I truly believed I was stupid and ignorant, and it got to the point that I would not speak in fear that somebody would "catch on to me." I thought they would notice how stupid and ignorant I was, so I kept my thoughts to myself.

I carried those feelings around until I was 51 years old when I hired a life coach who helped me to realize that I wasn't stupid or ignorant and, in fact, that I am a brilliant woman who has a lot to offer this planet. It was at age 51 that I started the personal development journey that would completely change my life.

With that said, something my life coach taught me is that I was the one who did all the work. While she was there to guide me and ask me the right questions to help me see 'my' right answers, I am the one who did the work. Why is this important for me to note? Because many of us don't give ourselves credit for the work we do.

When I was five years old, I ran away and was gone for an entire week. That was a strong and brave little girl to run away and be gone so long. But when I came home, I had my head bent down, my tail between my legs, and I was riddled with fear. I literally wouldn't look at people in the eyes for the next 46 years to come. Fear was debilitating and stopped me from living my life.

After working with my life coach, I decided to do something that would change my life. I had no idea what was in store.

I woke up the morning of January 1, 2015, and decided to break through one fear every single day for an entire year. Yes, I had that many fears.

I was no longer going to let fear control my life. I was taking a stand and was going to do something that would positively affect my life. And hopefully the lives of those around me.

What happened during that year is something that I never expected. The fears that I had were so deep rooted in the fear of judgment. As I look back in my past, I truly believe that my fear started in my household with the abuse from my dad and it carried forward with my ex-husband. The amount of mental and emotional abuse I went through starting at a very young age and continued with into my early 20s adversely affected decades of my life.

This was a pivotal time for me. Having the realization that my past controlled my future made me realize that I could change my present to also change my future.

We are so powerful as human beings. We don't give ourselves enough credit for what we can do. If you're finding yourself right now thinking that you don't have the fortitude or the ability to change your life, I'm here to tell you right now that no matter how old you are that you can change your life, and change your life for the better. It's up to you. It's your responsibility. No one else is responsible for your future.

You may have people in your life who are saying things or making you feel like you don't have the capacity or the ability to change. I'm here to tell you, again, that THEY ARE WRONG.

You get to choose your future. Will it be easy? Most likely not. Will it be worth it? Most likely yes. But you will never know if you don't take the steps to make it happen.

I spent a majority of my life blaming other people for bad things that happened and giving credit to other people for all the good things in life. That's because I didn't believe in myself.

It took me breaking through 365 fears. But it doesn't have to be that for you. You just have to make a decision to change.

You may need help with a coach or mentor, surrounding yourself with positive people in your life, making choices that are hard, making decisions you don't want to make, and simply changing.

There's a saying that, "If nothing changes, everything stays the same; the more you open your mind, the more you open to opportunity."

Are you willing to embrace change? Are you willing to embrace opportunities? Are you willing and open to making a positive impact in your own life and the life of those around you? Are you willing to step outside of your comfort zone and do something that scares the crap out of you just so that you can change your life? I'll tell you this, nothing happens without action. You can hope, dream, pray for, desire, manifest, anything you want in life, but if you aren't willing to take action, everything will stay the same.

The worst part? If you don't change, it's your choice.

I was reading Jack Canfield's book, *The Success Principles*, and the very first chapter was about accepting 100% responsibility for your life. I read that chapter in disbelief and, at the same time, awe. I was in denial. I did not want to believe that I was responsible for my life and where I was in my life at that time. Once I started believing that I am responsible, I started to embrace change. Everything in my life started changing and the more I accepted the changes, the more confidence I gained in myself and the more I released fear from my life.

Some people let fear stop them and others use fear to fuel them. One of the things I discovered while facing a fear every day is that I was one of those people that let fear stop me from living. Fear was controlling my mental wellness. Fear took over my life. And I let it.

As I head into my 60s, with knowledge and passion and drive and compassion and empathy and no longer being fearful of judgment, I am excited about the second half of my life. Second half at age 60? Yes, exactly.

When I was 13 years old, I decided that I was going to live to be 113 years old. That was in 1976, the United States' Bicentennial. It was such a fun time in my life that I decided to live to experience the Tricentennial. 113 years old.

In order to live to be 113 years old and to experience the Tricentennial the way I want to experience it, with full mind and body, I must have a tremendous wellness journey that keeps me mentally alive. That is one of my missions for the rest of my life. My other mission is to have as much fun as possible, hanging out with positive and uplifting people who are making a positive impact on the planet.

Knowing that I am 100% responsible for my life, it is my job and duty to find those positive and uplifting people so I can hang out with them. It's one of my favorite things to do, search for positive and uplifting people.

If you are one of those people and you'd like to be part of my life and my journey, let's connect. I'm all about raising the vibration on the planet so that we can experience a more positive life while we are here.

If you haven't already, are you willing to accept responsibility for your own life? If so, what are you willing to do in order to make that happen? What steps can you take to change your life?

One of the things I highly recommend is something that may sound simple, but may be difficult: DECIDE.

Yep, simply deciding is the first step you must take in order to change your life. Decide to be different. Decide to change your life. Decide to hang out with different people. Decide to make difficult decisions.

You may lose negative friends that you've known forever by making this decision, but trust me, as long as you keep your sights on the goals you have, you will never regret the positive changes that occur.

My mindfulness wellness journey has been nothing like I thought it would be. I am so grateful for that day that I raised my hand and said to myself, "I deserve this, I deserve better, I deserve to know who I am and what I'm all about. There must be more to life and I'm ready to dive in to see what that's all about."

Sometimes making a decision can be difficult and scary, but, as long as you know the result you want to get, and keep focused on that result, you will be glad you did.

I will close with this one last thing. The greatest gain I received from breaking through one fear every day for a year is that I realized that I must do things not in spite of the fear, but BECAUSE I'm scared. On the other side of fear is a great life waiting for you to jump in.

Go out there and live your life the way you want to live it. You are never too old to start something new. See yourself through the eyes of others, for others see the real you. You are brilliant. You have so much value to offer this planet. It's time you step into it and believe in yourself. We are waiting for you.

LYNDA SUNSHINE WEST

As the Founder and CEO of Action Takers Publishing, Lynda Sunshine West's mission is to empower 5 million women and men to write, publish and market their books to make a greater impact on the planet. She is affectionately known as The Queen of Collaboration. Lynda Sunshine is a Book Publisher, Speaker, Multiple Times International #1 Best-Selling Author, Executive Film Producer, and a Red Carpet Interviewer. At the age of 5, she ran away and was gone an entire week. She came home riddled with fears that stopped her from living. At age 51 she decided to face one fear every day for an entire year. In doing so, she gained an exorbitant amount of confidence and uses what she learned to fulfill her mission. She believes in cooperation and collaboration and loves connecting with like-minded people.

You can connect with Lynda Sunshine West here: www.actiontakerspublishing.com.

CHAPTER FOUR

STEP AWAY TO WELLNESS

by Sally Larkin Green
Creative Director, Action Takers Publishing™
www.ActionTakersPublishing.com

The best way I know to step up and be a winner in wellness is to step away and take the time to recharge. Many times, we become involved in drama that drains our energy. If that drama has nothing to do with us, or we are worried about something we have no control over, we need to learn to walk away. This isn't always simple or easy. We tend to have a fear of missing out (FOMO) and get caught up in situations we shouldn't be in.

Have you ever looked in the mirror and said to yourself, "I need to make a change and get healthier?" That's exactly what happened to me in March of 2020 at the beginning of the pandemic lockdown. I realized that while I was good at taking care of my business and my family, I was extremely bad at taking care of me. So, I decided that I needed to change. That one decision changed my life.

However, I was faced with an extremely vague goal. My journey to self-care was just that, a journey. I knew I would need to break that journey into small, achievable goals, so I did.

Following are the goals I set for myself and achieve them on a regular basis.

Step Away to Walk in Nature:

Have you ever noticed how good you feel after walking in nature? While it may take some persuasion to get you there, the question you might ask yourself is "Why does it make me feel so good?" One of the first things I began doing was taking daily walks with my husband and daughter. It was something new to me. I was always "too busy" to take time for myself.

Walking in nature not only improves your heart and fitness, but it also has measurable mental and health benefits. Walking has many proven benefits for your physical and mental well-being. It can help our physical body, but it can also improve our cognition, change our brains, and help us promote important practices like mindfulness and gratitude. All of this combined creates a perfect recipe to support us on our journey of mental health and wellness.

When I first began walking, I was out of breath after 20 minutes and had to stop every few steps while walking back up the hill to my house. After a few weeks it became easier and easier. I noticed that the head fog was gone, I was feeling less anxiety, and I discovered that walking is an inexpensive, low-risk form of exercise that when combined with nature and walking buddies, can be a very powerful and underutilized stress reliever.

Those daily walks have had such a positive effect on me and my family. If you are having problems with exhaustion, anxiety, or depression, I highly recommend adding "walking in nature" to your treatment plan.

Step Away for Quiet Meditation and Visualization:

Meditation is a way of managing stress and improving your overall health. Although it was something I enjoyed doing, taking the time to meditate and pray was not something I did regularly. As part of my wellness journey, this was a big piece of the puzzle. I would meditate in the morning before getting out of bed and again in the evening before going to sleep. It became a habit I really enjoyed and have continued. In addition, I added visualization. I often visualize my day or week.

Meditation and visualization are practical tools, often using breathing, silent contemplation, or prolonged concentration on something such as an image, phrase, or sound to help you release stress and feel calm and peaceful. Think of it as a mini vacation from the stress in life. Stress is your body's natural warning system. It releases a hormone called adrenaline which speeds up breathing and increases your heart rate and blood pressure. Taking time each day to meditate provides you with a way to manage stress in a healthier way.

Step Away for Naps/Go to Sleep Early:

Taking a nap was something I had never even considered. I was too busy for naps, and I had too much to do. Besides, naps are for kids. After our walks, I would often lay down and take a 20-minute nap. I was surprised at how much more rested it felt and how much energy I had afterwards.

I also found that going to bed earlier made me feel better the next day. The importance of getting enough quality sleep cannot be underestimated. Lack of sleep can lead to insulin resistance, alter appetite hormones, and reduce physical and mental performance, which can lead to depression, weight gain, forgetfulness, and accidents.

There are several things you can do to improve the quality of your sleep. First, avoid coffee, energy drinks, and other brain stimulants that may prevent you from sleeping. It is also important to ensure your sleeping arrangements are as quiet and comfortable as possible.

Step Away From Toxic People:

Have you ever spent time with someone and afterwards felt depressed, frustrated, or without energy? The people in your life play an important role in your health as much as your eating and exercising habits do. You want to surround yourself with people who make you feel happy and energetic.

We all know how important it is to stay away from "toxic" foods and alcohol, but what about toxic attitudes? Just like anything that is toxic, such as food or poison, toxic people can be extremely dangerous.

It is important to limit our time with people in our life who always have something sad, negative, or pessimistic to say in conversations and whose actions drain our energy. We often continue to associate with them because of guilt. It could even be a long-time friend or family member. We feel guilty for breaking up the relationship or breaking off communication.

One way I discovered to find uplifting, motivational people was by raising my hand and becoming part of a collaboration book. I was offered the opportunity and raised my hand and in October of 2020 I became a best-selling author with 150 of the most incredible people and I knew none of them beforehand. The friendships I have formed and the opportunities I have been offered have been priceless. You deserve to have people in your life that you enjoy spending time with. You deserve people who support and uplift you, and people you LOVE to hang out with.

Step Away From Social Media:

Constantly checking our social networks becomes a distraction and we often lose track of time. This was one area I was struggling with and needed to conquer to get my mental and emotional house in order. For instance, have you ever seen a post about someone who got their dream job, and you start questioning your career choice, or your cousin posts a political message and now you are mad at politics? For some people social media can be an emotional roller coaster of confrontation, perfection, and opinions. Taking breaks helps us to be happier and gives us time to do what needs to be done.

As part of my self-care journey, I began registering for online courses in sales and marketing. The time away from social media allowed me to concentrate on the classes and get myself into "learning mode" again.

Step Away From the News Cycle:

Constant exposure to negative news cycles is not doing your mental health any favors. If you spend all day absorbing news through emails, phone alerts, and social media, it will take a lot of your time and mental space. Once you get over the fear of missing out, moving away from the news cycle becomes easier. I have all the news channels blocked on all my social media accounts and disabled the notifications on my news apps. If there is a new story that I believe will impact me, my family, my business, or my community, I will investigate it. Give yourself permission to unplug from the news cycle and focus your energy on things you enjoy.

Step Away and Take/Plan a Vacation:

There is nothing like a good vacation and it is a great opportunity to escape from the daily grind and see new places, but these trips are also important in terms of your health and well-being. A vacation can be an opportunity to improve one's physical and mental well-being, so they are experiences that everyone should take advantage of at least once or twice a year.

As a family, we often planned staycations: multiple days off from work, social media, and obligations while staying at home ... even before Covid made it a "thing." I found that both vacations and staycations make a big difference in my production, energy levels, and self-esteem.

Step Away and Pursue a Hobby:

Finding a hobby or activity that brings you joy could be the key to a happy life. There's a saying, "All work and no play makes Jack a dull boy." Many people simply choose to participate in a hobby without being aware of its benefits. Many times, these activities help us to realize our greatest potential and shift our focus away from our problems.

I discovered a love for painting several years ago, and I have found that the hobby keeps me away from the refrigerator and snacking. These past couple of years, painting has helped me with the challenges of dealing with aging parents, financial difficulties, and stress.

Having a hobby sometimes gives us the opportunity to contribute to our communities. Whether it's basket weaving, painting, or building a birdhouse, our hobbies bring us joy and sometimes can even help us earn extra income.

Step Away to the Winners Circle:

Practicing a healthy lifestyle includes more than just eating right and exercising. It also includes spending time with yourself doing what you love. Stepping away is sometimes needed. The good news is that it is never too early or too late to adopt healthy habits.

Living a happy and healthy lifestyle is a puzzle with hundreds of pieces. Take it one piece at a time and you will begin to see the larger image take shape as you go! Get started today, make the decision, and you will improve your overall health and become a winner in wellness in no time at all.

SALLY LARKIN GREEN

As someone who was really good at taking care of everyone else, Sally Green looked in the mirror during the Covid lockdown and realized that she was really, really bad at taking care of herself. So, she began a journey of self-discovery, self-care, and saying "yes" to opportunities. She began eating healthier, walking regularly, and meditating more.

Since that time, Sally has become a 4-time best-selling author. She is the founder of The Self-Care Rockstar, where she helps women begin and continue their self-care journey with her laser coaching program. Sally is also the Creative Director at Action Takers Publishing, specializing in collaboration books that help women and men become best-selling authors. She has always had a passion for writing.

Sally lives in Connecticut with her husband and is an acrylic and watercolor artist.

Connect with Sally here: www.ActionTakersPublishing.com.

CHAPTER FIVE

RELIGIOUS OR SPIRITUAL: IS THERE A RIGHT WAY?

by Asma Yousif
Clarity & Confidence Coach
www.AsmaYousif.com

Am I religious or am I spiritual? What's the difference between the two?

"Religion is belief in someone else's experience. Spirituality is having your own experience"—*Deepak Chopra*

Here is an explanation showing the differences between Religion vs Spirituality according to ReachOut.com:

Religion: This is a specific set of organized beliefs and practices, usually shared by a community or group.

Spirituality: This is more of an individual practice and has to do with having a sense of peace and purpose.

Mindvalley.com references it more like a person and explains it this way:

The difference between a spiritual and religious person comes down to how they see God. For a religious person, the concept of God is predetermined, named, and comes with a set method on how to worship that God. A spiritual person, on the other hand, turns inwards to find their truth and finds God within themselves and all of life.

As a senior in high school in 1992, I came home one afternoon and my father greeted me with a grave expression on his face. Before he spoke, I knew something terrible had happened. He explained to me that Americans were singling out Muslims. Muslims were being viewed as "evil." This was terrifying for my family because being born in Iraq people assumed we were Muslim. However, my family and I are Christians. We were raised in a strict Christian household. Unbeknownst to me, this started my journey questioning the difference between religion and spirituality.

During this time, my family owned a Pizzeria that was doing really well until the Gulf War occurred. The economy was struggling, people reduced spending, and businesses were closing. Because of all the racism that was occurring against Muslims, my family was fearful. We were Christians, and in order to keep the family safe and protected, we openly shared our Christianity. We wore cross necklaces and had Christian items around the restaurant. As I look back at this now, I realize we were using Christianity to protect us against the racism we experienced during this time.

That was one of the first moments I used religion to protect myself against hate and judgment. The next memorable moment came on a day that America would never forget! The day the sky went dark and empty–September 11, 2001. When I awoke from sleep to the devasting news that New York had been attacked by terrorists, in my heart I knew my life would never be the same, as did so many others. However, for me, it's different. I am Middle Eastern. I was born in one of the countries America grew to hate. Even though I was born Christian and not Muslim, the American people wouldn't know the difference by looking at me. Once again, I began hiding behind my Christian religion by wearing a cross necklace to avoid stares, fearful looks, and hurtful comments. Even though I wasn't a true believer of the Christian religious doctrine, it felt "safe" to hide behind it during that time.

Within a couple of months, I stood up to the hypocrisy I experienced. I refused to hide! I started my spiritual journey knowing I had so much to learn. I opened myself to experiences and new perspectives.

To give context to this journey, let's go back a few years. When I was a little girl growing up in a strict Iraqi household, we had rules that were expected to be followed. My parents were religious people, and we would go to church every Sunday. My sisters and I would be in Sunday school, while the adults were upstairs praying at an Assyrian Orthodox Church. I didn't speak the Assyrian language, nor did I understand it. However, I was taught to believe in the same teachings as everyone at the church believed in. As a little girl, I had many questions. I was hushed any time I would ask anything about God or Jesus. I was expected to believe everything that was written in the Bible. I was conditioned to fear God and Jesus. I grew up thinking I was "bad" if I believed in anything different than what my parents modeled.

By the time I was in my mid-20s, I was constantly reading as many books as I could to learn about different perspectives about religion and spirituality. I soaked up anything I could find related to personal development. It took years before I was able to break out of the mold I was placed in as a child. I wasn't stuck in the religion, but was stuck in the confines of the religion. I continued to learn more and dive deeper into what religion and spirituality meant. I couldn't talk to my family about this for many reasons. They were raised in a way where this option wasn't available to them. Religion was a sensitive topic in our household; it wasn't discussed openly without judgment.

At first, I didn't have the courage to deviate from the Bible's teachings and listen to other people's beliefs. I worried "am I going to be condemned for the way I believe because it was different than what my family believed?" I didn't feel others had to believe the same as me. I was open and curious about other beliefs. My curiosity continued to grow. My soul just knew there was something so much more than what I was conditioned to understand and believe. I surrounded myself with friends who were spiritual, not religious. I asked lots of questions about their beliefs and dove deeper into learning. I was intrigued and desired to learn more. I became curious about other religions such as Buddhism, Muslim, Hindu, etc. I realized most religions have one similarity (often called "the golden rule"), which is to treat other people the same as you would like to be treated. This "rule" solidified my truth. I realized I don't need to be like other people to be powerful. It is perfectly acceptable to have different beliefs and still love one another.

I began questioning why we feel we have to be tied to one religion. Are we closing ourselves off from growth when we believe that we are right and everybody else is wrong? Does it make them feel powerful proving their religion is better than everyone else? What does that mean for people who don't have a religion they follow? Since religion is such a sensitive topic and isn't easily discussed amongst family, how do you find that harmony? These questions would repeatedly go on in my head.

I formed a bible study group so I could learn more about the bible. I talked to others who had studied it deeper and could offer explanations. The group I formed broke up after finding out I had no interest in getting baptized at the end of our study group. I felt very offended, judged, and unwelcomed by this group of "Christians." I thought, "How can I be outcasted by a group of Christian women who speak so highly of their church? They can quote scripture after scripture! Speak the Word of God, yet judge me and exclude me because I didn't want to be "born again?" Aren't we supposed to love everyone and welcome each person who is curious and asking to learn more? If we don't play by the rules, then we're kicked out of the game/church/religion?"

My emotions ran the gamut from anger, doubt, sadness, fear, judgment, sorrow. I questioned who I was and thought, "Why couldn't I just agree I would get baptized and become a born-again Christian?" I knew my heart and didn't want to live a lie just to fit in. What exactly was I trying to fit into? A world filled with judgment, self-righteousness, and restrictive expectations which is not how I wanted to live. Being born again would not elevate me. I have never viewed myself as better than the next person! But I consider myself a good person.

What does it mean to be a "good" person? Religious people might say that following and obeying the Word of Jesus Christ is sufficient. Most religions would suggest something similar. I believe there is no such thing as "good" or "bad." What is in our heart is what speaks volumes. I believe in karma, and it has a cause and effect.

If you wish or cause harm to others, you bring harm to yourself.

If you have hate in your heart, hate will reveal itself in your life.

If you have love in your heart, love will show up in your life.

If you are grateful for what you have, doors will open for you.

I trust myself, God, the Universe, and my Spirit Guides that everything will work out FOR me! When doors close it's because there is a better one that is getting ready to open. If I do not get what I want or there are obstacles in the way, it is because God is protecting me from what is behind that or what it could be. As long as you keep trusting yourself, praying, and surrendering the Divine/God/Universe/Spirit will deliver and guide you. When we realize we do not have any control over things in our lives, surrendering comes easily. The only things we can control are our behavior, how we respond to situations, and how we make others feel when we interact with them.

I have a couple of close friends who taught me so much along my spiritual journey that helped me understand these revelations. I discovered that it's okay to not be tied to one religion, or to any religion for that matter. I began to understand God in a different way. I realized that God lives inside me and is not separate. This created awareness, healing, and connection within myself through self-care, self-love, and self-acceptance. Once I started loving and accepting myself, I became connected with the Divine, who in my eyes is God, the Universe, and Spirit. I learned for me in order to live a happy, fulfilled life, I must show up in love and gratitude! For me, God is LOVE!

Living life with love in my heart towards everyone I meet has changed so much. I am now at peace with myself. I am no longer afraid to be vulnerable with others. I don't fear having intimate conversations with people I don't know well. I am open and free in the knowledge I am not going to be judged or "condemned" because of the choices I'm making in my life if I do not follow a specific religion. If someone attempts to do that with me, I choose not to accept it. One of the most empowering realizations of knowing my worth is that standing up for my truths is what has set me free. Freedom awaits you too!

This freedom is the reason I choose to live my life with love and gratitude!

I still identify as a Christian; however, there is a caveat to that. I was raised with Christian roots, but I'm equipped Spiritually as well. I hold the same beliefs without the control and doctrine of religion.

I believe God lives within me in the form of LOVE.

I am LOVE!

I am GRATEFUL!

This is the path I have chosen for myself. As for the question of Religion or Spirituality, in our home, we have chosen to teach our children that God lives inside our hearts. In our home, our golden rule is having love and gratitude for everything and everyone around us.

If you are in the circumstances of questioning like I was, I suggest:

- Be courageous
- Ask questions
- Find a mentor with an open mind

- Always be open to transformation
- Accept that change is inevitable!

We are never stuck! Whether you choose organized religion, spirituality, or someplace in between, know that freedom is the prize!

ASMA YOUSIF

Asma Yousif is a Clarity and Confidence Coach and is currently working on her certification in Holistic Body Wellness. She has been involved in personal development for many years and her curiosity with the human brain has enhanced her talents. Asma believes that what we tell ourselves represents the life we're living. She supports men and women in their personal and professional lives to reclaim their life which they had been living in avoidance and embark on living a life by design and purpose. We do this by shedding layers and years of pent-up anger, self-sabotage, fear, judgment, comparison, and perfectionism to arise into higher ways of living. Her mission is to heighten millions of beautiful humans across the globe and enhance their pursuit of living with greater purpose, clarity, and passion.

It is important for Asma to help create new pathways of thinking, believing, living, and breaking down generational barriers that weigh us down.

She believes that leaders effectively lead when emotional wellness is achieved.

You can connect with Asma here www.asmayousif.com.

CHAPTER SIX

FROM FAT TO FIT—IT STARTS WITH THE MIND

by Bryan Allen-Smith
Owner, Allen Enterprises
https://linktr.ee/Bryanallensmith

"Fat." It's a word I've heard a lot and a word that I've had negative connotations about most of my life. I grew up in a small town where everyone knew everyone, and everyone knew what everyone was doing. Yeah, one of those towns where you had to fit the mold and needed to do everything you could to <u>not</u> stand out.

I struggled with my weight for as far back as I can remember, and I have vivid memories of having to wear jeans that clearly had husky written on the back label. I also remember feeling like I was labeled, and that people were judging me daily for my weight. I wondered why a company would call pants for overweight boys "husky" size. It just didn't make any sense to me, but it was my reality and the reality of so many others in the '80s. I was insecure in my own skin and it took me a very long time to realize that most of my insecurities were in my mind and not reality. While I was overweight, I was the one struggling with it and it wasn't taking much mind space for others. As a matter of fact, most didn't even care or even notice. This led me to discover that mindset is so important and something that we have complete control over. I've also learned that the word fat isn't negative. Fat is a part of us all; it's part of our DNA. A long time ago, a guy at a gym I was occasionally going to shared a story with me about fat, and he said, "fat makes you fat, eat less fat and you will see results." I've hung on to that for a very long time and think of it often as I am preparing meals or making food choices. There is good fat and there is bad fat, and we constantly make the decision about what kind we want in our bodies. Almost all of my life I was choosing bad fat because, well, I loved fried foods, soda, snack cakes – all the things that I knew were bad but tasted so good.

For most of my life, my weight has been a rollercoaster. There would be moments where I'd focus and lose weight then I'd gain it back (usually more) just to do it all over again. It was a vicious and endless cycle that I had. "I love food." There, I said it. Food is my lifeline, my comfort, my go to on a bad day, and a treat on a great day. Food and my obsession for delicious food controlled me for a long time. I ate to survive but I mostly ate because I loved the taste. Honestly, sometimes it still controls me but my mindset has allowed me to better control it and make better choices. It's allowed me to enjoy food now and get excited about creating masterpieces that taste amazing but are also amazing for me.

About seven years ago, I met a great friend and mentor. She introduced me to a lifestyle change process, a routine that allowed me to fill my body with premium nutrition every morning. She shared something that has drastically changed my life. I need to provide some context into how I was living before this change, however. I was busy, well super busy. I worked a demanding job that had me supporting 14 coffee shops in a large metropolitan market and we were growing and changing so much so that my time outside work was limited. Well, that's what I thought at the time. I really had lots of time, but I didn't have the energy to realize it. I had to wake up early every morning and it was tough. I'd hit the snooze button on my phone three or four times before I'd finally roll out of bed and begin my day. I'd shower, get dressed, and head out the door. My days always began with a fatty breakfast sandwich, full meal with fried meats and cheese or breakfast burrito and coffee. I'd work all day eating high calorie snacks and drinking sodas to finally swing through a fast food drive-through to get a large size combo on my way home. I'd eat and do some work on my computer while sitting on the couch until I fell asleep watching TV, usually the Food Network. Finally, I'd wake up in the early hours of the morning and stumble to bed where I'd sleep until it was time to do it all over again. This was my daily routine for several years and, while I knew I wasn't happy, it was my life. Thinking back, I acted like I was fine, but I don't think I was. I was frustrated and tired and really just going through the motions.

It didn't take long before I hit my highest weight of 350 pounds. I was fat and I felt it. I was tired of being tired and knew I needed to do something different—introduce my friend and an opportunity to do something different. I remember asking myself, "How long will this last? Will this be another loop in the rollercoaster that I've been on for so long? Will this actually work?" By this time, I was working on my mindset and the importance of telling myself positive things and not focusing on the negative thoughts that would pop in my head. Well, it took a lot of work, but I finally believe I cracked the code on consistency in mindset and I'd like to share a couple of best practices that I apply to my life daily. First, however, I need to provide insight into how these changes and practices changed my life.

It began great and remains great. I remember waking up my first morning excited and knowing that I wanted this to work. I completed the three steps I needed to do and began my day. I got through the day like any other day, drinking coffee while watching what I was eating. That first evening, I felt a little more energy than normal and cooked dinner. The next day, I repeated the routine, and by mid-day I had so much energy that I couldn't believe it. I asked myself, "Is this real or is it in my head?" Day by day I had more energy and found myself doing more. Within a few months, I was in my zone and I was running two 5k's per day, eating healthy, drinking only decaf coffee and water, and had begun losing the weight that had accumulated over all the prior years. As my journey continued, I lost more weight and finally reached my goal of 185 pounds. I was loving life and finally living the life I deserved. I was on fire. It's been great because I haven't missed a day of my routine for seven years. While I have experienced a few bumps along the way, I have never felt better and now I continue to focus on my positive mindset daily. I still wake up every morning and do what I need to do to achieve my goals. I still follow the routine that began seven years ago. I am so thankful that someone thought enough of me to share their story, their journey, their struggles and, most importantly, their routines for success.

As I shared earlier, there are a few best practices that I've applied to my life that have helped me get out of the fixed mindset of being a 'victim of fat' to having a growth mindset on how the fat that I have is the fat that is supposed to be within me.

- I begin each morning telling myself that I am going to have a great day. When my feet hit the floor, I ask myself, "Bryan, what will you do today to conquer the world and make an impact?" I keep that top of mind throughout my day. When I find myself overwhelmed or in a situation that causes negative thoughts, I take a moment to pause and reflect on what's possible and how what I do in that moment will help me achieve my life goal of making impacts.

- I ask myself daily, "What's possible and what can I do today to make an impact?" because how you think affects what you will achieve in life. We've all heard the old adage, "If you think you can, you can; if you think you can't, you won't." So, wake up and tell yourself something like I do and you, too, can conquer your world. Create positive affirmations for yourself, I have them on my bathroom mirror.

- When you get in a rut and start having a fixed mindset, you have to change your thoughts or you will never achieve your goals. If you think that you are not good at something like I did with my weight journey, you start believing that you will never be good at it. Stopping and rewiring the way you think by sending different thoughts to your brain will help you overcome the victim mentality and allow you space to know you can achieve anything you desire.

- Our brains have the ability to evolve and change. It was once thought that the human brain stopped developing in childhood. While this has been debunked over the years, having a fixed mindset can lead to creating roadblocks that stop you from growing. Being open to new ideas and being positive allows for growth and allows the brain to learn and grow.

- It's going to be hard work and it's going to take time for anyone that wants to create a growth mindset and live life to the fullest. Having a growth mindset will create pathways for reframing the way you approach challenges, problems, and skills. If you put your mind to work and don't give up, you will achieve success.

Thinking back to those early years of my life where I believed that being fat was negative and that the world saw me and judged me negatively helped shaped me into the person I am today (pun intended). Don't get me wrong, I do have my moments. Some days it's harder than others to stay positive and harder to focus on growth vs fixed thoughts. Others can quickly change your mood, but I've learned if I allow that to happen, then they have control over me. No one in life needs to control you. You have one life, one story to tell and it's yours. I'm sure there are people that still judge me and people that may still think I am fat, but that's okay because I am who I am and I know the work I've put in to get to where I am today.

Life can be anything you want it to be if you tell yourself that it can be and put the work in to achieve your goals. By adjusting the way I approached life and creating routines that allow me to create processes that give me the structure to succeed, I now have the space to have a growth mindset. Next time you want to achieve something, ask yourself how you can grow in the moment. Ask yourself what is possible. I do this on a daily basis and this has given me the ability to be a better person for myself, for my husband, for my family, for my friends, and for those I work with. I choose to live awesome and my goal in life now is to help others #liveawesome2.

BRYAN ALLEN-SMITH

Bryan Allen-Smith has been in direct sales and leadership roles in major corporations for over 25 years. He has been a top producer in several companies and honed his skills while working with Starbucks for over 13 years in a senior leadership role. While he still works in corporate America, his passion for cooking has led him to becoming a Director with the Pampered Chef. Bryan is currently working on a project to develop and launch a program called "Build a Better YOU" in Fall 2022. The program will help participants tap into their strengths and identify ways to live premium. In his spare time, Bryan loves cooking, learning, spending time with his husband and family, loving on his pets, thriving daily, and living life to the fullest. He wakes up every day with a mission to give more and be better today than he was yesterday. Bryan believes that everyone deserves to live life to the fullest and uses the hashtag #liveawesome2 as the focus for his work.

Connect with Bryan at https://linktr.ee/Bryanallensmith.

CHAPTER SEVEN

RECIPE FOR A FULFILLED LIFE: A GRATEFUL HEART WITH A SIDE OF GRACE

by Cynthia Adams-McGrath
Author, Poetess, Caregiver

It's August of 1983. I'm six months pregnant with my first biological child and something doesn't feel right. My mother's instinct kicked in. I was blessed to have a bonus daughter, Kim, which provided somewhat of a parenting training ground, but couldn't have prepared me for what lay ahead. I wasn't an alarmist, but I was filled with worry. After much contemplation, my husband at the time rushed me to the emergency room. I was examined by the emergency room doctor and informed that I was in active labor. It was too soon to have my baby, but he was determined to make his appearance. It's hard to imagine, but this traumatic experience was the beginning catalyst of my journey to living a fulfilled life with a grateful heart. It's been a recipe developed over time and with very specific ingredients.

The first ingredient became evident during this trying time. That ingredient is accepting challenges and allowing them to help you grow. I was gripped with fear. What if it was too early and my baby didn't make it? Our local hospital was not equipped to handle a premature birth. Therefore, I was prepped to fly out by helicopter to a Virginia hospital. The nurses urged me to stay calm for the sake of my baby.

I thought, how can I stay calm? I took my hands and rubbed it over the small mound under my rib cage. I closed my eyes to pray saying," Please God, take care of my baby."

As I rolled out to the helipad, the summer heat smacked me in the face. This made it hard to breathe. The helicopter blades were deafening as they put me into the helicopter. This took fear to a whole new level. I could only think of my precious cargo that I was carrying and if my baby was going to live or die.

After an uneventful flight, 24 hours later, after an emergency C-section, I was a new mom to a 2-pound 6-ounce baby boy we named David Aaron Walters. They showed him to me briefly, then rushed him to the neonatal intensive care unit to be cared for. Not surprising, because he was very premature. Joy was mixed with trepidation, but I was a new mom. I never expected it to be this way, though. Wow! I was overwhelmed with gratitude that my son was still here and alive. I knew that we would have a battle going forward, but I trusted my faith in God to carry us through.

Unfortunately, since I had a fever, I was not able to see my son for forty-eight hours. It felt like weeks. I was really growing impatient. I wanted and needed to have time to bond with my son. On August 17th I finally decided I was going to go to the neonatal intensive care unit on my own to see my son. I gingerly climbed out of bed, took my I.V. pole in hand, and went to the elevator. Unbeknownst to me at the time, I was supposed to tell the nurses if I was leaving the floor. It didn't matter, though, because I was on a mission to see my son. I had so many emotions inside me: love, fear, happiness. My brain was on overload as my heart fluttered with excitement to see my little miracle.

When I got to the NICU, I put on a yellow gown and gloves and went inside. There were so many babies who had machines beeping and lighting up. It was a little disconcerting at first, although I did understand the machines were giving the nurses vital information about these critical babies. The nurse asked for my name and my son's name to which I responded Cynthia Walters and David Walters. Here I stood as a first-time mom at 26 years old with a baby who was critically ill. I hadn't even begun to understand the magnitude of what that would mean.

The nurse looked at me and said, "Are you sure you want to see him?" I was stunned by her question and said 'YES!'

"He could die, you know," she responded in a very flat tone.

I firmly responded, "Please take me to see my son, David."

She brought me to his isolette. I took a deep breath as I gazed at this tiny human. I had birthed this little human, my son. There were tubes and wires attached to this 2 lb 7 oz of baby.

His crying sounded like a newborn kitten, soft though strong. This is not what I had expected as a new mom. I pondered, "Where is that cherub looking face with chubby cheeks?" I put my hand through the opening and touched his tiny fingers. I said to him, "Don't worry, son, your mom is here." I made that commitment and I have kept it. I bowed my head to say the Lord's Prayer. My son was clinging to life; furthermore, I was so grateful for him even in his frail state. We would fight this battle together.

David showed me what a fighter looked like as he continued to battle typical preemie problems. Those included breathing issues, heart complications, and a brain bleed, although David kept bouncing back. There were babies who were healthier than he was that passed away. It was heartbreaking to see. After eight weeks of rollercoaster medical issues, David Aaron Walters came home on October 22, 1983, weighing five pounds two ounces wearing Cabbage Patch doll clothes.

As David grew, I noticed he wasn't achieving his developmental milestones. I reached out to our local Early Intervention Educational resource specialist who provided me with the name of a hospital that could evaluate David. We made an appointment at A. I. Dupont in

Wilmington, Delaware, to find out what issues he might have. David was eighteen months old when we had him examined by a multitude of doctors. We sat down with them so they could discuss their diagnosis.

"Mrs. Walters, your son has Cerebral Palsy."

Cerebral Palsy?

My words were all running together in my head.

"What exactly is Cerebral Palsy?," I said as tears came rolling down my face. The doctors began to explain to me that it was a neurological condition that happens sometimes with premature babies. This was a diagnosis that I knew would change both our lives forever. It was a mentally and physically exhausting two-hour ride home from Wilmington, Delaware, to Cambridge, Maryland. I knew my son had a condition that would last his entire life. This isn't something he will outgrow or overcome. I was overwhelmed by this thought and it wasn't something I expected. What was I to do now? Am I strong enough? I was a 28-year-old woman with a husband, teenage daughter, and a son with a disability. I was thankful that I had a diagnosis. I was grateful I knew what I was dealing with so I could formulate a plan. After everybody was settled in bed that night, I got on my knees and prayed to the Lord. I prayed for his help and guidance then thanked him for giving David to me even with all the challenges that would lay ahead. This leads to ingredient number two: Equip yourself with knowledge.

It was time for me to be my son's advocate. That meant seeking out the knowledge I needed to serve him. I needed to find out all I could about Cerebral Palsy. This was all pre-internet, so I went to the library, though information was pretty scarce. I called the early intervention team, again through the Board of Education. They referred David to physical therapy, occupational therapy, and mobility specialists. David was depending on me. I vowed I was going to do everything in my power to be the best mother I could for my children. I began to formulate a plan.

This led to ingredient number three: Extend grace to others whether they want it or deserve it.

Concurrently, I evaluated the status of my marriage, only to admit it wasn't viable anymore. I was so grateful that he provided me with David and my daughter. He gave me everything that he was capable of. Along with a disabled child and a teenager, I couldn't handle an adult who disabled himself with alcohol. David had a total of 19 surgeries, and his father was there for them all. When he arrived with alcohol in his backpack, I gave him grace to be who he was in David's life. David needed his father, so I accepted him for who he was. That ingredient has been one of the most important in my life. The extension of grace to someone is as important for them as it is for you.

With that decision, I was divorced 33 years old with two children: a teenager and a child with Cerebral Palsy. I decided to move forward with my life and do something for myself. This involved ingredient number four: Extend and give grace to yourself. I decided to go back to school. This was an extra dose of ingredient number two–educate yourself. This decision helped me feel more confident as something other than a mother. It was so great to be around my peers and feel a sense of routine. I'd been isolated for so long caring for David. I felt fortunate to be able to learn about something other than medical terms and equipment. I brought David to a couple of classes with me so he could see how hard I was working to be more independent. I was the mom who brought her kid to her school instead of dropping her kid at school. Usually it's the other way around. This made me chuckle. I was grateful to be able to show David how committed I was to attain my goal. I graduated with honors from community college in 2010 with my son and parents by my side. It was important to have my parents there. With a disabled child, they feared I might not ever complete my education. However, I persevered and earned an Associates of Arts degree in human services.

After the graduation, David looked at me and said, "I am so lucky to have you as my mom." With my eyes full of tears, I cupped his face with my hands, and said, "David, I am so thankful to the Lord for giving you to me. I am the fortunate one."

My life was moving in a positive direction even considering all I had faced. At that point in my life I was ready to allow someone to love me. In 2010, that blessing named Kenny arrived. Embracing the past challenges, failed marriages, and lessons learned, it revealed ingredient number five: Always find joy. Find joy, even in the most difficult circumstances. It was time for me to allow myself grace yet again, because I deserve love. Eleven years later, I am so grateful to have this man love me exactly as I am.

I believe I've always had the recipe for a grateful heart.

What's the recipe for a grateful heart?

1. Accept challenges and grow through them.
2. Educate yourself–whatever that looks like for you.
3. Give grace to others when necessary.
4. Give grace to yourself always.
5. Always find joy–even in difficult moments.

Accept the challenges, mix thoroughly, and allow them to move you forward. Find joy and whisk it into unexpected or unpleasant situations causing gratitude to rise. Be able to give and receive grace to all which will allow you to be truly grateful. Learn as you grow and sprinkle with kindness. It's done perfectly when joy radiates from within.

As I continue this journey, I intend to continue to follow this recipe for a fulfilled life! Perhaps it will become a family favorite for you, too!

CYNTHIA ADAMS-MCGRATH

Cynthia Adams-McGrath was born in Salisbury, Maryland. Her current home of thirty-eight years is in Cambridge, Maryland. She resides there with her husband Kenny of eleven years and her son David. David is thirty-eight and has Cerebral Palsy and is a true light in her life. Her daughter Kim and family live in Florida. Cynthia received an AA degree with honors in Human Services from Chesapeake College in Cambridge, Maryland, in 2000. She has been a member of Choptank Writers Group in Cambridge, Maryland, since its inception. She has had two pieces of poetry in the magazine, *Imagine The World as One* the Spring edition of 2021. She is an accomplished writer looking forward to publishing her first book in 2022.

You can connect with Cynthia on Facebook here: https://www.facebook.com/cynthia.a.mcgrath.

CHAPTER EIGHT

SOCIETY AND STATISTICS DON'T HAVE TO DETERMINE YOUR FUTURE

by Dara Bose
Owner, FireWife Boutique
www. FireWifeBoutique.com

My mother was only 17 years old when she became pregnant with me, and my father was 25. They married before I was born. We lived in a trailer park in a rural town just outside of Springfield, Illinois. My dad worked for the United States Postal Service and my mother dropped out of high school and was a stay-at-home mom. When I was around three and a half years old, my sister was born. Even at the young age of three, I could tell that money was tight for our family and adding another mouth to feed only brought more stress and tension between my parents.

One night, as my parents and I were sitting in the living room watching television, there was a loud knock at the door. My dad got up to answer and I saw the look of terror on my mom's face. I was only about four years old, but I knew something was wrong. As my dad made his way to the door, my mom quickly moved me to the bedroom just around the corner from the living room, where my little sister was sleeping. She shoved me into the room and told me to watch my sister. When my dad opened the door, there was a dark figure with a deep voice standing there. As the man and my dad talked, I could tell that they were not friends. Their voices got louder and louder. My mom then left us in the room and in typical four year-old fashion, I peeked out to see what was going on. Just then, my sister's empty bassinet came flying towards me and hit the wall. Then, I heard the man say, "If you don't pay me what you owe me, I'm gonna kill your wife and kids and make you watch, before I kill you!" This is the earliest vivid memory that I have.

My dad was a drug addict and had not paid his dealer. Of course now I understand that my dad's drug addiction is part of the reason that my parents fought and why money was tight. My mom did an amazing job of protecting us for my dad's addiction and divorced him shortly after I finished kindergarten. Now, don't get me wrong, my dad had his demons, but he was still a good man and a great father. Both of my parents remarried, and both continued to struggle financially throughout my childhood. I did not grow up on the *right side of the tracks* and we were definitely in the lower class of the town where I grew up.

Being the daughter of a drug addict and a high school dropout teen mom, the odds were stacked against me. Society and statistics would say that I was predetermined to be the same as my parents. But I used my past as a learning experience and decided that I wanted something different for my life. I started working at age fourteen and continued to work through high school. In my junior and senior years of high school,l I worked two jobs in order to save for college and my future. I graduated high school at seventeen and enrolled into college. I bought my own home at eighteen, but really did not know what I wanted to do and found that paying for my own schooling while trying to support myself was too much. So I dropped out of college and just worked at jobs that paid the bills. At twenty-one, I married the love of my life and we are about to celebrate our twentieth wedding anniversary.

My parents' choices did not get to determine who I am; I got to CHOOSE! Your past does not predict your future and neither do your current circumstances. As a life coach, women come to me all the time with self-limiting beliefs (these are beliefs that are so rooted in your subconscious from past experiences that they will hold you back from the things you want). These self-limiting beliefs can seem so matter-of-fact in your own thoughts that you do not even realize you have them. Sometimes things happened to them and sometimes they do things or make choices that they regret and they let those past choices and experiences determine their future. Your past only tells you where you have been, not where you are going. If you took a wrong turn, you can still get to your destination, it might just take you a little longer. If someone flattened your tire, you don't have to flatten the other three. If you took a detour, you just have to decide to get back on the road.

Don't discount your past because it gives you wonderful lessons. Your past is an abundance of unrefundable gifts and you get to determine how you use them. I like to look at life as a road trip. There is a starting point and an ending destination. As you travel along, you may make a rest stop, take a back road, and you may even take the wrong exit because you were following bad directions or got distracted by some fancy billboard. But, ultimately, you are in the driver's seat.

Knowing where you have been is important because you can decide whether you want to visit it again or if it's something to be left in the rear view. But you also need to know where you are. Take a good look at your surroundings and who and what you have in the car with you. Most importantly, you have to know your destination. If you don't know where you want to go, you can find yourself driving around in circles, or spinning your wheels.

When I was thirty-two I gave birth to our third child. After struggling with infertility, my husband and I were so excited to have a little girl to add to our family. We already had two boys and having a girl was a true blessing. Then we realized that we would have two children in daycare and I was working at a job where I was miserable. So, we decided that I would leave my job and become a stay-at-home mom. Our route had changed. We shifted our lives and made things work.

However, it was not long into my new stay-at-home mom gig when I found myself feeling like something was lacking. I love my kids, but I needed something else. I needed more.

A close friend was going to have an opening in her office for an accountant and it would pay very well. So, I decided to go back to college and get a degree in accounting. I was always good at math, so I figured it would be a great profession for me. Once I had completed my degree, the original job was not available so I took a different job, and then another, and another. I still felt like something was missing. I felt unfulfilled. I figured they just weren't the right one. Then I landed my "dream job."

It was the first day of my dream job. I felt that I had finally made it! After spending the majority of my adult life in a revolving door of jobs, I had expected the doors to open, doves to come flying out. and a choir of angels to sinnngggg. Of course that didn't happen. The first couple of months were amazing! But in less than a year's time, I began to feel the emptiness again. The darkness of my depression and anxiety began to creep back in. But, why? I had the big office, the fancy title, and the nice paycheck. It was the 'one thing' I thought I needed to make me happy, to fulfill me.

Instead, I found myself dreading going to work, stressed, gaining weight, and to get really honest here… drinking more than I care to admit. I felt defeated. I was in a downward spiral and losing myself along the way. It was affecting my family. I was lashing out at my husband and losing my temper with my kids. I knew I needed to do something because of my history with depression and my genetic predisposition to addiction. The path I was going down was dark and I was struggling to see the light.

Then one evening, as I was self-medicating with a bottle of wine and Facebook, I happened to scroll past something and it was as if someone had finally turned on the lights! I had been searching for the '**one thing**' that was going to make me happy, a new hobby, that new direct sales company, or that "dream job." But, I realized there was no "ONE THING" that was going to make me happy! I was the one responsible for my happiness! It comes from inside me. I could CHOOSE to be happy!

Society told me that I should be happy. I was happily married, had three kids, a nice house and car, and a good paying job. And the fact that I still felt unfulfilled, I thought that I might be broken. Maybe I wasn't supposed to be successful and happy because my dad was a drug addict and I didn't grow up on the right side of the tracks.

But, I wasn't broken! I realized that I was trying to fit myself and my happiness into someone else's definition of success. I was trying to use someone else's map!

I had not taken into account, ME! We all have a different story and our maps do not look the same. Our starting points are different and even if our destinations seem the same, they are different. We have to take into account all of our past experiences that make up who we are, our likes, our dislikes, and all the things in between. You have to define what success is to you. What lights you up on the inside? What fills your cup? What brings you joy?

My first memory of a drug dealer threating to kill me isn't something I want to relive all the time, but it is something that helped to shape me and is part of the filter I use to view life and make choices. I have learned to let go of the things that I cannot change and use the lessons I have learned from them to help me move forward. Forgive those who have wronged you and forgive yourself for the things you have done. Holding onto the past doesn't help you move forward.

Stop living life looking in the rear-view mirror because you will crash and burn. Take a moment or two to glance into it to be sure your past is still there, but keep focused on where you are going. Take the time to stop and enjoy life. Most of all, be sure that you are sticking to your own map and heading toward the goals that bring you fulfillment and purpose because you deserve a life of abundance and you are meant for more!

DARA BOSE

Dara Bose is the owner/operator of FireWife Boutique, a certified NLP Practitioner, Life Coach, best-selling author, and public speaker. She has spent years working on personal development while reaching top rankings in the MLM industry. Through her work in MLM, she discovered her passion for building up other women and her purpose to help them thrive. The wife of a firefighter and mother of three, Dara never ceases to amaze with finding time to support and uplift women in her community. Whether through participating in small groups at church, organizing fundraising events, and everything in between, Dara represents her best self in all she does. She motivates women to seek their best self through self-reflection, motivation, fashion, and friendship. Women seek out Dara for guidance regularly when working through difficult times, or just needing the support of another woman/mother/wife/business owner. Constantly seeking to better herself and provide the best support she can to others, you can always find her reading a book or attending seminars that build her up and better equip her to share her messaging.

Dara is best known for a saying she uses regularly with her children and friends and can also be applied to anyone in most all situations – "But did you die?" Most importantly, Dara wants all women to know, you are worthy, you are beautiful, and you are meant for more.

You can connect with Dara here: www.firewifeboutique.com.

CHAPTER NINE

MENTORS MATTER

by Darryl A. Johnson
Founder & CEO, Thriving Women Network, Inc
www.ThrivingWomenNetwork.com

It is biblical passage that "for as he thinketh in his heart so is he" and I wholeheartedly believe that "Mentors Matter." My question to each reader is, "Do you believe that mentors matters?" It is not my opinion but factual that if you interview the most successful people in the world, one habit that they have in common is retaining a formal and informal mentor. The role of mentors as a catalyst for success is becoming increasingly clear and it has become my life mission as a mentor to share why mentors matter and encourage people to seek them out.

Have you heard that Mark Zuckerberg, Founder & CEO of Facebook, started to receive mentoring from Steve Jobs, Founder of Apple, when Facebook was experiencing a rough patch in the company's early days? Zuckerberg was invited to Jobs' temple in India to reflect and reconnect with his vision for the company, and the pair continued to have a mentor-mentee relationship and friendship until Jobs' passing in 2011. When Jobs passed away, Zuckerberg took to Facebook to express his fond admiration for Jobs, writing, "Thank you for being a mentor and friend."

Bill Gates, Co-Founder of Microsoft, credits the scale of his business success to the mentoring he received from Warren Buffet. In 2015, Gates wrote of Buffet in his own blog, "Warren isn't just a great friend, he is an amazing mentor. I have been learning from him since the day we met in 1991."

J. J. Abrams, at the age of 16, won a young filmmaker award and was hired by Steven Spielberg to help clean some of his old movies and transfer them to tape. Spielberg was so impressed by Abrams work that a long and prosperous relationship ensued with Spielberg as his mentor and they went on to direct blockbuster films like Mission: Impossible III, Cloverfield, Star Trek, Super 8, and Star Wars: The Force Awakens.

Nevertheless, if you were like me growing up in the inner city of Chicago, the word mentor was not in your vocabulary. My mother raised 8 kiddos without a husband, so getting trusted advice was hard to come by. Generally, I received spiritual coaching from the Bible and Elders in my Church, but when it came to money and business, I was clueless. I remember watching the Oprah Winfrey Show in the late '80s when she invited her 4th grade teacher, Ms. Duncan, to the show to thank her for being a great teacher. Nonetheless, the word mentor did not connect with teacher or coach to me, maybe because my mother did not allow us to play organized sports.

Not until later on in life when I attended a network marketing meeting at Transamerica Life did the word mentoring became an empowering word. This prompted me to research the word mentor and to my surprise it was defined as an "experienced and trusted advisor" like a teacher, parent, or coach. At that moment, the word mentor came back to me, and I realized that when I was in high school my woodshop teacher, Mr. Smith, was my mentor because he encouraged me to develop my talent as a craftsman, enlightened me to participate in the Chicago Industrial Arts Fair, and empowered me on how to win several achievements in the arts. Mr. Smith never used the word mentor even though he gave me mentoring advice like, "Plan you work on paper and work your plan off the paper" and treated me like his son.

In retrospect, I honestly believe my successes and failures in life and in business have been directly linked to listening to trusted and experienced mentors (or the lack of listening to them) before making decisions. To illustrate my phenomenon on mentors, I am going to share two of my personal life stories with different outcomes with the goal of enlightening, encouraging, and empowering you to seek mentors. My mission is not to tell you why you need a mentor or even how to find a mentor, we will cover that in another chapter. My purpose in writing this chapter is to share my personal experience in hopes that it resonates with you when making decisions.

My first story began when I was 17 years old. I woke up from an unconscious state lying in the middle of the road in Chicago to the realization that I was in a motorcycle accident. Staring down at me with tears in his eyes was a man asking me, "Are you okay?" I attempted to stand, but my lower half would not move, the pain from my dislocated right hip kept me on the cement pavement. My vision was blurred due to the bruise on my head, but I was able to turn my head to the right and I saw my motorcycle. Then, turning to my left, I saw my older brother lying unconscious on the pavement in a coma. Almost immediately, my memory came back to me, and I started screaming at the man standing over me, "Why did you make that U-turn?" At that moment, my life changed forever, and I remember my mother saying, "I don't want to feed you from a straw," which was her way of saying to me the risk is not worth the reward.

You may be thinking, accidents happen, and you would be correct. Notwithstanding, you may also agree that the outcome would have been different if I listened to my mother (experienced and trusted advisor). We can all agree that it is not enough to just have the GPS app, we must use the GPS navigation system to keep us from getting lost, save us time and get us to our important destinations as quickly as possible. Similarly, my decision at the young age of 17 to buy the motorcycle without the recommendation and support of my mother directed me down the path of more risk and because my brother did not have his safety helmet on before the accident, he died 14 days later of a brain hemorrhage. I struggled for years trying to gain wisdom and understanding of my decision at this young age. Nevertheless, this life lesson taught me the value of seeking wisdom (the soundness of an action or decision regarding the application of experience, knowledge, and good judgment), which I did not process at the time of my decision. We as mortal humans tend to rely on our inner emotions and peers, instead of pausing to have mentoring conversations with experienced, trusted advisors before making important decisions. I realize that sharing this story will touch someone's heart and that is the responsibility of a mentor. Let's move on.

My next story began at the age of 23. I was newly married and working for the Chicago Board of Options Exchange and the Chicago Sun-Times part time to pay my bills. I maxed out my first Visa credit card to buy furniture and had no life insurance or emergency fund. Eventually, I was promoted on my first job to Market Analyst, which allowed me to quit my second job, but it only replaced the money I was making part-time with the Chicago Sun-Times. I began seeking other employment, but my non-college resume held me back from securing a higher paying career. Coincidentally, my mother-in-law introduced me to this married guy named Bobbie, and after meeting him he mentioned that both him and his wife were employed by the U.S. Postal Service and had started a business part-time. My first impression of Bobbie was that he is making great money, maybe he could get me and my wife employment at the post office.

Nevertheless, Bobbie wanted to share with me and my wife a financial needs presentation on how to buy low-cost life insurance, establish an emergency fund, and invest in mutual funds for retirement. Considering my dismal financial situation, I told Bobbie that I was not in the position to make any financial decisions or buy any financial products at this time. He did not allow that to stop him. He asked me if I would be interested in getting my license and certification as a Financial Coach part-time so that I could earn more income? I told him that working on commissions was not a smart decision and my wife would not agree to me being a salesman.

I would like to say Bobbie gave up trying to mentor me, but he didn't. He was so excited about his business, and I was so negative about my finances. Eventually, I decided to listen to his presentation and purchased a Life Insurance policy but refused again to join his business. I asked him how much commission he made from my life policy. He hesitated and told me about $300.00 dollars and at that moment I was shocked because I was taking home from my employer about $600.00 every two weeks, and he made $300.00 in one hour. The following week he told me my uncle purchased a Life Insurance policy from him and I started calculating his commissions in my head and it really started to bother me that I was not moving on the opportunity.

You may be thinking like me, everybody is not a salesperson and maybe I should go back to college and get my degree, and you would be correct. Nonetheless, I was not listening to the mentoring that Bobbie was providing. As a mentee, I told him my problem and as a mentor he provided me a solution, but I was not willing to follow his GPS. Think about this, Bobbie was already gainfully employed with the Postal Service, and he was willing to mentor me on starting my own business as a Financial Coach providing financial education to families. What was stopping me?

Sadly, I found myself rejecting the mentoring that I really needed. I was not willing to be uncomfortable and vulnerable to learn something new. I struggled with the idea of working on commissions and teaching others something that I was struggling with. A few weeks later, Bobbie invited me to his local office to meet his mentor and once again I rejected the offer. Finally, something happened on my job that prompted me to review my options, I got laid off from the Chicago Board of Option Exchange. Fortunately, I found another job working at Household Finance but, ironically, they required me to study and take the state life and health insurance examination to keep my job and I did not hesitate to conform. When I think about my nonconforming mindset, Bobbie was trying to get me to get my license to start my own business for months, but I refused.

After passing my pre-licensing test and earning my state license, I became the top salesman at Household Finance. A few months passed before I spoke with Bobbie and, at that time, I mentioned to him that I no longer was employed with the Chicago Board of Option Exchange but received my life & health license. He was excited for me but hesitated before asking, "What is your commission contract with Household Finance?" I proudly told him 14% on Life Insurance products. Bobbie gave me this grin that I will never forget and said, "Darryl, our starting contract is 40% and you can promote yourself 100% in a couple of months if you work hard."

Immediately, I told him that I was interested in meeting his mentor and getting my contract. On November 28, 1988, I met Bobbie's mentor and joined A.L. Williams Corp the same day. Bobbie's persistence and mentorship made a difference and I appreciate him every day. I am celebrating my 33rd year as a full-time entrepreneur and, like I mentioned at the beginning of this chapter, "Mentors Matter."

In honor of mentors like Bobbie Richardson, I decided to pay it forward by creating the Trendsetter Mentor Group in March of 2014. Our mission is connecting people and their passions and 2,000 members later I wholeheartedly believe that we are Mentors and are making a difference.

DARRYL A. JOHNSON

Darryl Johnson started his career in financial services at the Chicago Board of Options Exchange as a Price Reporter in 1983. In 1985, the stock market crashed and the opportunity to work in Market Regulations as a Market Analyst opened and he earned his promotion.

He left the Chicago Board of Options Exchange in 1988 to work with Household Finance Corp. as an Account Executive and earned his financial service license during his short tenure. He left HFC in 1988 and joined an MLM company called A.L. Williams Corp after learning about the concept of Buy Term & Invest the Difference. This opportunity gave Darryl the financial education and freedom to build his own company within a company. ALW was sold in 1990 and Darryl joined Capital Choice Financial Services in 1997.

In 2014, his passion for mentoring and coaching was amplified when he created the Trendsetter Mentor Group on Facebook, which led to creating an online school for Financial Coaches called Pivot Point. In 2019, the mission of enlightening, encouraging, and empowering women for growth and success led to creating the Thriving Women Network due to the outpouring of support from women from around the country. In December 2021, Darryl and his team signed a contract with E360TV to stream Talk & Reality Shows that impact viewers to become their best version.

You can connect with Darryl here: www.ThrivingWomenNetwork.com.

CHAPTER TEN

STRESS KILLS... AND LOSING ONE MILLION DOLLARS SUCKS!

by Debbie Morton
Founder, Success With Debbie
www.SuccessWithDebbie.com

Fortunately, I didn't die from stress. However, I did lose a million dollars and it really did suck.

I'll never forget the day I came home from running errands and asked my husband how his meeting with his new financial advisor went. With his head low, he quietly whispered, "Somewhere between horrific and catastrophic."

My heart sank because, in that moment, I knew our suspicion was confirmed. His entire retirement account of nearly $800,000, (EIGHT HUNDRED THOUSAND DOLLARS or 8 tenths of ONE MILLION DOLLARS) was gone in what we learned was a brilliantly executed Ponzi scheme that lasted over 12 years.

Fortunately, I had a small retirement account of around 200K, so it's not like we were destitute; or so I thought. Four months later, I received a call from the FBI and learned my 401(k) account was also gone and they wanted my help with an investigation. Just like that...poof, my retirement was gone, too (ONE MILLION DOLLARS TOTAL).

At that time, I had just closed a brick-and-mortar home care business to launch a new career where I could earn income from my phone or computer. I longed for a stress-free business with no employees, no inventory, no overhead expenses, and no government or insurance agencies knocking on my door everyday with their hands out wanting to be paid. I wanted simple. I wanted a laptop lifestyle with just me and my wi-fi and the ability to earn income from anywhere in the world.

I was 56 at the time and my husband was 66 and had been retired for 12 years. We now had VERY little money and no income other than his social security. We were embarrassed by our bad financial decisions and kept our situation a secret from friends and family. Neither of us wanted to go back into the workforce knowing we could NEVER earn back what we had just lost working our 9 to 5 jobs.

As I closed the doors of my home care company, I made a $3,000 investment to learn how to generate leads through Facebook sponsored ads. My plan was to use these skills to grow a network marketing business. I assured my hubby everything would be all right. I convinced him I'd build a team by generating leads online, and we would be fine.

Have you ever bought a course or took on a project that seemed like it would be easy, only to find out it's anything but? That's what happened with this course. I diligently watched the videos, created the webpages I'd need, then set up my Facebook ads as instructed - and got zero results.

It wasn't until I went to a three-day summit offered with this course that I realized there was a lot more to learn. Convinced I could shorten the learning time if I just joined a one-year mastermind for $18,000, I did what any logical (make that desperate) person would do. I bought the mastermind. I figured I was already about 100K in debt, so what's another 18K?

I'd love to say the investment in that mastermind delivered what it promised. It didn't. Although I was one of the most successful students in the mastermind class, I barely made back my investment in it let alone enough money to actually live on. I was more confused and frustrated than ever.

A year older and deeper in debt, I was anxious, scared and I had a knot in my tummy 24/7. I thought success was what would make the knot go away. What I didn't realize at the time was the knot had to go away for success to happen.

While that first $18,000 mastermind didn't deliver what it promised (a fast track to a six-figure per year online business), it was the best investment I ever made.

It led me on a journey of personal development. It connected me with other people who gave me coaching opportunities. It opened doors to other trainings, courses, and masterminds and each gave me more skills, more confidence, more exposure.

The journey to success is rarely, if ever, easy. It takes struggle, persistence, learning new skills, tenacity, consistency, and stepping way outside your comfort zone. And that's just the beginning. For most people wanting to succeed at something, it's easier to give up than to push through the pain. That's why so many live in a world of mediocrity.

I didn't have a choice to do anything but push through the challenges.

I did NOT want to go back to work for corporate America where I spent the first 20 years of my career feeling trapped and giving my talents and skills for a fraction of what I knew they were worth.

I did NOT want to own another brick-and-mortar business with all the stress and all the risk that goes with it.

I created in my mind what my future would be and began taking action. When I hit roadblocks, I adjusted my course and kept moving forward. When I felt like giving up, I didn't - I dug deep and kept going.

Today, I am a leader, a coach, and a mentor to thousands. I've shared a training platform with entrepreneurs like Kevin Harrington (the original Shark Tank Judge), James Malinchak (Big Money Coach and ABC's Secret Millionaire), and Les Brown (International Motivational Speaker).

I lead a team of entrepreneurs and I'm committed to helping them have the success they want and deserve, without suffering through the struggles I went through.

There are many lessons I've learned in this 5-year journey to success that I'd like to share. These tips will work for you for whatever you want in your life: Better health, better relationships, more prosperity, etc...

When You're in the Midst of the Struggle, Don't Focus on the Struggle.

Focus on where you want to be. Remain laser focused on that goal. Know that every challenge is shaping you into who you are meant to be so you can help others in the way you're meant to help them.

The universe is perfect and everything happens for a reason. There were so many times I couldn't understand why everything was so difficult. Why courses I bought didn't work, why companies I joined went out of business, why other companies I joined operated with ethics I was not in alignment with. Looking back, I was on the road I was meant to be on. Each failure was a lesson. Each challenge made me stronger and I would not be able to help the people I help today had I not experienced what I did.

Think About Your Thoughts.

There is an ongoing never-ending conversation that is happening in your mind. The bad news is that 80% of those thoughts are negative. The good news is two thoughts can't occupy your mind simultaneously and you have the ability to change your thoughts when you learn to think about what you think about.

When a negative thought enters your mind, acknowledge it. It's your brain trying to protect you so it's doing what it's supposed to do. Then, consciously override that thought and replace it with a better one. Instead of thinking, "It'll never work," change that thought to, "What will it take for this to happen?" Instead of thinking, "It's so hard to lose weight," think instead, "What am I going to do today to weigh less than yesterday?"

Consciously changing your thoughts from negative to positive will put your mind in a space that can create the actions necessary for you to succeed.

Beware of the "Yeah-buts."

Yeah but, I'm too old to start a new business. Yeah but, I'm an introvert. Yeah but, I don't have the right skills. Yeah but, I'm not pretty enough. Yeah but, it'll probably never work. Yeah-buts will take you down. Stop them at all cost and focus on "I am." I am successful, I am a healthy person, I am an amazing mother, etc. Thinking "I am" instead of "yeah but" will align your conscious and sub-conscious mind to take positive action.

Listen to your "buts" and change them to "and." Instead of saying, "I want to start a new business BUT I'm old," say instead, "I want to start a business AND I'm old." The "but" prevents you from taking action; the "and" opens your mind to possibilities you might not otherwise have considered. Instead of saying, "I want to lose weight BUT I hate the gym," say instead, "I want to lose weight AND I hate the gym." Now your brain can create alternate solutions like going for a bike ride or a hike, instead of the gym.

Ditch Your "To-Do List."

Success doesn't happen overnight. You can't lose 50 pounds overnight and you can't create a six-figure income overnight.

Success comes from little, consistent actions you do every day.

"To-do lists" create overwhelm. So instead, create a "power list" of 5 things that you are committed to getting done each day that will make you feel like you won the day. It won't change your situation overnight. However, little by little, it will move you towards an ultimate goal while enjoying incremental wins every day.

If you miss a day, that's okay. Just commit to winning tomorrow, the next day, the day after, and so on…

I've listed ideas for what you might want to put on your daily power list. Keep in mind that when something on your list becomes a habit, you can replace it with something else that you want to work on.

Here are some ideas to get you started.

1. Read a personal development book for 30 minutes
2. Meditate, do affirmations and/or mantras
3. Write in a gratitude journal
4. Eat healthy
5. Drink "x" amount of water
6. Workout for a minimum of 30 minutes
7. Spend a minimum of 1 hour of quality time with your spouse, kids, or a friend

Those in business might include…

8. Post on social media a minimum of once per day
9. Connect with at least 5 new potential prospects
10. Make a minimum of 3 follow-up calls to prospects
11. Give 2 or more presentations
12. Send an e-mail to your list

Hopefully you can see that each of these are minor tasks, but they often get overlooked because the day gets away from us. If you commit to just 5 things, you will win the day more often, lower stress, and make consistent progress toward any goal you have.

Live in Gratitude.

Science has proven that gratitude reduces stress and depression, and improves overall well-being. Instead of thinking about what you don't have, think about all the amazing things that are in your life right now. Be grateful for the food you eat, the roof over your head, the car you drive, your friends and family, your education, and all the other things big and small. To be truly successful, you must live a life of gratitude. I recommend keeping a journal and add to your list every day.

My story isn't one of rags to riches. After losing the million dollars, we were somehow always able to earn enough money to pay the bills, as long as we tightened the purse strings when it came to extravagant expenses, so officially we never wore "rags."

Today I live an abundant life and live in gratitude for our million-dollar loss because, had that not happened, I wouldn't be where I am today.

I have new skills, confidence, community, and I get to travel the world earning income from my phone and my laptop.

We can't control what happens around us in this thing called "life;" we can only control our attitude.

Wherever you are in your journey, if you want more, you can create more.

Be the victor, not the victim.

Decide today who you want to be, who you want to inspire, who you want to empower. Create that vision, take action, and say to yourself and to the naysayers around you, "I Can, I Will, WATCH ME!"

DEBBIE MORTON

After 20 years in corporate America, Debbie Morton decided she would rather work for herself than others. She left her 9 to 5 to buy a failing business that she later sold for 10 times her original investment. She has owned 2 brick and mortar businesses: a metal finishing shop (Powder Coating) and a senior home care franchise.

She's a Diamond leader in the network marketing space where she coaches and mentors thousands of entrepreneurs both on her team (TrifectaELITE) and within the entire company.

She was a top producer in two affiliate marketing companies which led her to be a high ticket closer for numerous "online gurus."

She is an expert in personal development training, online marketing, sales training, and personality training. Instead of DISC, she teaches similar concepts using four birds, which is far more intuitive than letters or colors.

Debbie's passion is helping others succeed. During her entrepreneurial journey she's invested hundreds of thousands of dollars in business ventures, courses, and masterminds. Some worked and were valuable, others didn't and provided valuable lessons.

Whether you're just starting in business, a solopreneur (trading time or products for money), a business owner (leveraging efforts for residual income), or seeking to learn how to preserve and grow wealth through investing, her passion is to help you achieve all the success you are willing to work for.

You can connect with Debbie here: www.SuccessWithDebbie.com.

CHAPTER ELEVEN

THE PATH WE'RE ON IS UNCLEAR UNTIL IT'S CLEAR

by Dionne Roberts
Founder of The Virtual Holistic Centre
https://thevirtualholisticcentre.com

My mind was all consumed by the noise of the vacuum on the colorful Turkish rug when I was stopped by the vibration of my phone that read, "Dad is in hospital, he's had a stroke." Silence descended upon me, accompanied by a stab, right up from under me.

With my right hand between my legs and my left just below my navel, I tried to stop myself from falling to pieces. "Argh," I cried out, as I doubled up, holding my fallen belly. No one came to my aid. Switching off the vacuum, I laid on the rug, in a fetal position. Mentally deciding what to do while waiting for the pain to subside.

Seven years prior, my mother also had a stroke. Once able, I travelled for hours across town. With my body that was crippled with pain hours earlier, but was now held together by numbness. I believed I walked into the hospital's bay, not feeling my legs. Eyes wide, lost, and glazed, scanning the room until they froze, over my left shoulder at the sight of his heart shaped face, complete with a silver goatee beard, I raised my eyes and looked into his, which usually glistened, but were now dim. As if a dial had been turned down, it was apparent he had lost more than his strength. He had lost his most valued asset, freedom!

He looked small, yet still he filled the bed as he greeted me with a muffled slur of "hello daughter." As I moved closer, I sensed his fear. Could he possibly be scared of me? So, I opened my heart and began to fill the silence with questions of "what happened" and sympathy. Before I left, I said, "I love you," and his response was, "I know." I saw this look of fear, for a further eighteen months. Each time it arose, I felt frozen. I didn't know how to reassure him that I wasn't going to treat him the way he treated me nor did I know how to approach the conversation of his immortality.

Upon his hospital discharge, each family member tried to pressure me into taking care of him. After all, I am the eldest daughter of six children within the household I grew up in. I was single and didn't have any children, and even though I've been the main caretaker for our disabled mother for five years prior, it didn't count. The thought of being locked up again with another disabled person freaked me out. I tried to extend my ability. After all, he is my father, but the reality of that was no comfort. Instead, my mind and body could not distinguish the fear of the present and the fear I felt growing up with him.

The more time I spent with him, the more old wounds resurfaced. Which led to conversations we never had before. When he eventually apologized for leaving me, he said, "I'm sorry, but it was just business," which made my heart ache, my body hurt, and my head fuzzy. I became more withdrawn and I shut down. "Is this what living with him is going to be like?," I wondered.

It was clear to both him and I that I should not be his sole nursing care provider. Meanwhile, the pressure from the family intensified as their actions became relentless with the constant phone calls, in-person arguments, and tricks, like not turning up to cover my shift. Seeing the role I had inherited in the family he left me to raise, he said, with tears rolling down his face, "If you don't go, I'm afraid you'll have a stroke yourself." Although I was grateful for his blessing, I, too, began to cry.

I needed to establish some boundaries with the rest of my family, so I headed to my friend in London. As I traveled, I felt a weight had lifted. Although I had to share the details of what was going on. As to why I was on the run, including parts of my childhood for substantial evidence, given that he is a lawyer. His company helped me feel safe and rooted again.

Even though I didn't sleep well that night, I did expand out to all four corners of the bed. As I was now free! And could breathe. I laid in the middle of the purple sheets with my hands on my belly feeling the disconnection of my parts; I hadn't realized the lumps just beneath my hands had grown to the mass of a cantaloupe melon. Parasites which had taken up residence and were nothing more than the sum of my memories, visitors who had overstayed their welcome.

That morning, over a couple of poached eggs, I explained to my host how I have fed them, held them, and wrestled with them all my life. But last night changed everything. From this day forth, I was done with them. The veil had been lifted and I was finally ready for the big 'H,' that's right, a hysterectomy.

When I returned home, I would visit my father every third day, liaise with his doctors, accompany him to all his hospital appointments, as well as the care team at the residential home. One day, when I was taking him to this hospital, my phone rang. It was the women's hospital. A woman said, "Dionne, I have an emergency appointment for you in two weeks." Alarms bells went off in my head, "Shit just got real." I explained how I needed more than two weeks to get things in order. So we agreed to extend it another four weeks. The extra time meant I could plan how best to ask for help. The nurse who prepped me said, I couldn't go home for a month, after the operation.

The big question lingered in my mind since the day I made the decision to have the surgery. I went back and forth, mentally processing how I was going to go about asking for help. Thinking about everyone's life, their schedule, and how it would affect our current relationships, how will I go about asking for help?

The first person I asked was the person whom I call my substitute father, the one that took care of me when I had the previous surgery, an embolization, a procedure that cut the blood supply to my fibroids so they would die off and get discharged from my body. This left me with one more person to find, for weeks three and four. I also needed to make plans for when I returned home. I knew I had to tackle things differently. For example, not to expect the people I've always been there for to be there for me. Not to arrange for one person to do it all. As it's vital they don't feel overwhelmed, or backed into a corner, unable to say "no." So I decided to send my family a group email, cc'ing in everyone.

I placed all my good friends in a WhatsApp group, from the closest (who no longer live close by) to my new friends near where I lived. This way I was not asking anyone in particular. Instead, I put it out into the universe and waited to see who would step forward. Straight away one of my close friends offered to take care of me (for the second half of that vital month). Another offered to go with me to the hospital. This role had many nuances to it. I had envisioned a person being there when I woke up, to help me with my morphine, and to stay until we found a nurse willing to help me in the same way for the duration of that first night. Due to having trauma leftover from previous surgeries, I needed someone to nurse me every two hours.

My friend who accompanied me ended up being there from six in the morning until after ten in the evening. A job I originally planned on splitting between two people, but no one felt comfortable with medication or seeing me in such a state. I was fully aware of how much time she sacrificed and the courage it took for her to hold my hand through it all.

Having spent the first month away from home, I was eager to return, especially to my own bed. At the start of the fifth week, my closest friends began rotating their visits, traveling from various cities across the country. One of them gave me a sound healing session with tuning forks, which calmed the internal, erratic shaking in my body. It also had a positive effect on the pain. I had no trouble falling asleep that night—the first since the operation. A few hours later, I woke up in pain and with heat as if I was on fire from the inside out. It became apparent I had a serious problem with sleep, having prematurely entered menopause.

The following day I recalled the relaxation technique called Yoga Nidra (an auditory experience one listens to). I laid there in preparation in a cold sweat with six blankets waiting for a hot water bottle to arrive. Before the kettle reached boiling point, I had stripped down to my vest, and had sweat dripping off my eyebrows. Once she pressed play on a recording, the extreme heights of my temperature fluctuations began to curb. Like magic, the technique calmed my body, like the sound healing did the night before. The difference is there's no need for the presence of a therapist. It directly gave me a sense of reconnection to numerous parts of my body. Awarding me with a sense of wholeness. For the first time, my mind felt like it had a part to play in my recovery. This made me feel good about myself, while positively impacting what was going on in my body. The recording invited my mind to listen and my body to follow along, carrying out the instructions, which consist of being still, never moving externally, but internally working.

In between their visits, my new friends popped in, washed some dishes, bought me a meal or took me shopping while protecting me from the potential knocks, from strangers that would have caused excruciating pain. But I didn't always have that luxury. I got the news via text that, "Dad is not expecting to last another 24 hours."

I spent my last moments with him performing a Buddhist tradition called a transference of consciousness. Once I saw his gaze had lowered, I quietly left. I wish I could have stayed into the night, but being twelve weeks out of surgery I could not stay up all night in a chair. After I got home and settled into bed, I received the news that my father had died in the middle of the night.

The loss of my father and my womb were not the only deaths my body and mind were dealing with. I felt as if grief had become a new skill of mine. Now I'm only reminded from time to time. Another reason why self-care is ongoing for a woman who has had a hysterectomy, besides not to activate the casual catalyst of the reason behind the surgery. For some women, the trauma of the surgery itself may be the catalyst that triggers another condition. Therefore, the fittest and happiest one can be, before the surgery the better. Women need a considerable amount of support for this undertaking and if she can be free from financial stress, then it will serve to stop the stress hormone from raising war, causing damage during the recovery process.

This experience influenced me and my business. Which is why I trained in 'Yoga Nidra' which translates to the 'Yoga of Sleep.' I further developed the technique by creatively weaving healing modalities into the ancient healing art form. To deliver transformation on a physical, emotional, mental, and spiritual level, I use this methodology to help women where I was some years ago; to embrace rest, repair, and feel rejuvenated. As I guide them through conquering unhealthy patterns and establishing new mind-blowing habits that reignite their vitality. I hope this chapter has helped you, in some way to do just that.

DIONNE ROBERTS

Dionne Roberts is known as the 'Sleep Whisperer' because she specializes in a sleep technique that gives you the benefits of two hours of sleep in just twenty minutes.

This holistic entrepreneur has been a holistic practitioner for over 25 years and now she primarily helps menopausal women and hysterectomy survivors who seek rest, repair, and rejuvenation so they can conquer unhealthy patterns and establish new mind-blowing habits that reignite their vitality in support and celebration of their new bodies and minds.

After graduating at the top of her class, she is on a mission to help these women. Furthermore, she helps wounded healers by supplying a virtual space known as 'The Virtual Holistic Centre' where they can collaborate, receive support for themselves while serving women and impacting the lives of others, as they manifest change in both health and their professional lives.

Dionne loves helping people. Being the eldest daughter of six children, it's her innate nature to care for others. Having trained as a professional contemporary dancer in her youth - anytime she was benched, she would massage her fellow classmates. Little did she know, this gift, given to her as a child, would become her future career, paving the way for her healing practice.

To connect with Dionne Roberts, visit https://thevirtualholisticcentre.com where she will gladly assist you.

CHAPTER TWELVE

HIDE AND SEEK - IT'S A CHOICE

by Jaymie Hale
Reiki Practitioner, Natural Lifestyle Educator
www.facebook.com/jaymie.halengoupa

We always have two choices in life; Hide or Seek. I have spent a great deal of my life in hiding. I am not ashamed of that. It's just a fact - not good or bad. We can hide or we can seek the truth. I choose to seek the truth, my truth. Not the version someone else believes our truth should be, but MY truth as I know it. I like to think of truth as light. I will always be on a quest for greater understanding and knowledge–more light. I continue to seek my truth and be a light in the world even when it doesn't make sense to others. Even through all the challenges (darkness), I am eternally grateful for the life I have, as I believe it offers opportunities to learn and grow closer to a place of true peace and joy. The summer of 2021 presented a new challenge.

What is going on? I awoke with excruciating abdominal pain and went into the fetal position and dialed 911. An ambulance ride to the ER, and a CAT scan later, revealed gastric issues along with some other issues that resurfaced from the past. Summer of 2021 and it seemed I was plagued with yet another health journey. I say another journey, because my previous health challenges required me to seek out information and learn about my own body very early in life. I learned there are reasons that health issues occur. They don't just appear. After exhaustive research, it provided me with clues. Contrary, however, to what medical professionals had previously suggested was the cause. Anxiety was the typical answer I was always given. The silent but obvious answer of "It's all in her head." Were they right? It didn't feel right. Fear is intruding and keeping me anxious. I don't want this - how can it just be in my head? Even though I felt like hiding again, I chose to continue to seek my truth and move into the light. The light is where peace, joy, and harmony reside for me. This journey started many years before that summer, however, with my mother's help.

One of my earliest memories is me as a sweet-natured, yet highly rambunctious 5-year-old little girl named Jaymie, who was endlessly curious. That curiosity and a burning desire to learn would serve me later in life on this journey. However, at five years old, I exhibited behavior that was concerning. This became problematic in school. I was the 5-year-old that couldn't "sit still" in kindergarten. This, coupled with depressive manifestations, was unusual behavior for someone so young. My Momma's heart (and gut instinct) told her this wasn't right. The journey to finding natural care alternatives and answers for my health issues started with my mom. She refused to medicate me. She searched for natural alternatives to medication very early in my life. She was always encouraged by her mother to search for natural solutions. She didn't believe medication would be my answer. I am grateful for that belief and have steered clear of medication as much as possible in my adulthood, as natural options became my personal health philosophy.

Fast forward a few years and a major family trauma coupled with puberty, and I decided to push away from the natural medicinal protocols that had drastically changed my young life. Unfortunately, this created another round of seeking more help and answers as I became sick again. Two severe episodes of mononucleosis left me weary in my tracks. Each episode was a journey back to health. I learned more about natural medicine and clean eating - this time I did the learning. I became obsessed with label reading and watching anything that went in and on my body. This has included everything right down to my laundry soap. I gave up the dream of becoming an author, as I had hoped to do for a long time because I felt like I hadn't gotten my story perfectly in order yet.

I'm still in the recovery period from a diagnosis a few months back of Lyme disease with comorbidity. This simply means there are multiple health problems present at the same time. I am choosing to disclose these issues because someone, somewhere is sitting in silence and suffering. I've likely had it most of my life.

However, even with the challenges this illness has created, these very words are fulfilling a lifelong dream of becoming a published author.

I write this to encourage you that we are all on a journey of healing. We are all at different stages of our journeys. I want to focus on the unseen side to my journey. The spiritual, mental, and emotional side of illness. It's the one we hide. It can feel embarrassing and create feelings of shame or unworthiness. This is the part that causes people to hide in the game of life. Once again, always two choices, Hide or Seek. Sometimes it's difficult to explain when you "look" fine but you don't "feel" fine! This describes the largest portion of my own health journey. There are theories that suggest physical ailments are the result or manifestation of "hidden" or repressed emotions. Others often see our scars and bruises in us before we do. After searching my entire life for answers (picking up in adulthood where my mom began in my early childhood), I feel there is validity to this school of thought. I am a single mom to two precious young children who have been greatly affected by my health concerns. Yet I won't give up seeking.

What fuels me onward towards achieving my maximum health are my children. God is my guiding light and they are God's precious little rays of sunshine that illuminate the darkest recesses of my soul. When I've felt overwhelmed, like I'd never "arrive," I look to my higher power. I use the word God here, some say Universe, Source, Divine Light, Creator, Energy, or Truth. Define that entity or "place" within you however suits you best. For me, that is God and I will use that term going forward. Go to that space when you seek refuge or truth, and need gas in your tank to fuel your journey. Be still, quiet, and sit with Him. Drink from His waters and be refreshed. The next leg of your journey won't seem so difficult. Remember to LISTEN. This voice is your guiding light and will lead you to your truth. Always listen intently! There have been countless times during my life that those thoughts and feelings of overwhelm threatened to take me down. God and those little rays of love have helped me seek my truth rather than continue to hide. Hide and seek isn't a simple child's game. It's the game of life! It's a daily choice to hide or seek the truth/light. With chronic illness, it can be very appealing to hide behind a label or diagnosis. Ironically, the act of hiding creates a barrier to healing.

Even when weary from mental or physical challenges such as Lyme disease, you are NOT your illness. You are not the life you "find your-self" in the midst of right now. You are not your circumstances. What you ARE is perfection - a piece of "creation's jigsaw puzzle," as we all are. We are here to learn and grow and stand in the light. YOU are not sick… you may FEEL sick, but that's different. Chronic illness is only an attribute, not who you are. It's a temporary state; NOT your identity.

What pushes you onward when the hours and tasks ahead feel so very bleak and daunting?

Each person living with a chronic or serious illness can benefit from a "source" from which to draw their strength, determination, and inspiration. Especially during those times of greatest trials, this source strength is imperative. Get still and quiet. Allow the light to grow in you. God and my children are what creates the light for me.

Some things require time and quiet to manifest. Be patient on your journey of healing. Most importantly, be patient with yourself. You are not in competition with anyone. Choose time with yourself. It's not selfish - it's self-care. Schedule alone time and you will be able to heal easier. This quiet time will help you understand that in order to fully come out of hiding, you must choose YOU! Alone time will block the distractions of the world and allow you to become better acquainted with the fabulous creation that is YOU. If you want to care for others - you need to care for yourself first. It's like on the plane when you are flying with children - you put YOUR oxygen mask on FIRST, so you can serve your child. Surround yourself with a network of people who support you fully as a human being. As the light in you grows, you will illuminate the path for others.

Since receiving a Lyme diagnosis and understanding its effects on my body and mental health, I have taken that necessary time to heal both physically and emotionally. I have also become more compassionate for others. Life can present us with some pretty hard knocks... IF we choose to see them that way. I work hard to reframe things and see them as growth opportunities. This path of walking with Lyme disease has been a very challenging one for myself and my family. In many ways, my children have been affected most during this journey. I am fiercely independent and I was required to ask for help. I am typically known as an extremely private person, rarely sharing personal details (that's the hiding part). Writing this is a HUGE leap of faith for me! Why share such personal information?

My only intent is to help or inspire someone who is still hiding, knowing it's okay to step into the light - to be the light. If I can encourage ONE person to seek information and truth, it is a win! Seek the light. Hiding in the dark only multiplies those negative emotions. That negativity fuels illness. Trying to seek the truth WHILE hiding doesn't work either. I have tried it for years. If my challenges and pains can offer hope and inspiration to someone, it all serves a purpose. I pray my candid story and painful remembrances can inspire, teach, or offer some light that it does get better. If I have a weak moment, I reach to that support system I have built and my higher power to guide me back to the light and encourage me to come out of hiding. If I keep hiding, I am teaching my children to hide as well. I AM committed to teaching them and whoever is reading this to seek your truth and live your life in the light with no shame! The greatest gift I can give to this world is to raise my two beautiful babies into happy, healthy, light-exuding souls by exuding light myself. They will in turn encourage others to follow the light and seek the truth. Surround yourself with others who understand choosing yourself is the solution. Keep the tiny flame of hope inside lit and keep searching, seeking your truth and light.

Your truth is perfectly yours.

QUIT HIDING!

Your truth is your light! Seekers don't stop looking for the light. They BECOME the light.

JAYMIE HALE

Jaymie Hale is a spiritual seeker, devoted mother, lover of all things natural, reiki practitioner and gentle soul. As a first-time author, she is passionate about providing a read that will encourage and inspire those in need of reassurance. She is a teacher and a light for those who are on a journey through life challenges. As a constant seeker of natural modalities, she inspires others to join her in creating a more natural lifestyle and spiritual growth for a true sense of peace, joy, and love.

You can connect with Jaymie here:

https://www.facebook.com/jaymie.halengoupa.

CHAPTER THIRTEEN

COVID 2020: LOVE LOST .....AND FOUND

by Dr. Jeffry G. Lapsker, DDS
President, Dr. Jeffry G Lapsker
www.sleepwelljoliet.com

They say that in life, sometimes timing is everything. Well, for me, having the opportunity to write this chapter couldn't have come at a better time. You see, I've been writing a screenplay about my life, in my head, for the last few years. When 2020 came along, we all found ourselves living very strange lives. Nothing was the same. The "new norm" was not normal at all, but that's what we all needed to follow, and we all had a story to tell.

For me to actually put pen to paper and share an annotated version of my life is very exciting and fulfilling. I hope I'm able to convey my joy, my pain, and in the end my newfound strength and love of my own life and of the world around me. I've always believed that things happen for a reason, and my story should be a great inspiration for anyone who thinks that too many roadblocks have been put in front of their path to happiness. As long as you are alive and keep an open mind, you'll be surprised where the journey will take you.

I always had a desire to be in the healthcare field. Right out of high school I was accepted into a 7-year medical school program. However, as I got further into my education, I became less enamored with becoming an actual physician. For many reasons it was just not for me. I was taking too much sickness and death to heart. I became somewhat of a hypochondriac. The hours were a total polar opposite to my natural biorhythm sleeping schedule. Nothing felt right and it was time to make a change

The hospital where I was studying had a dental wing. I spent time volunteering there and observing this new world. I loved everything about it. The attitude of the doctors and staff was very uplifting. I had to make a major life altering decision at 21 years old, and I did. I spent the next few months sending out applications to dental schools. No matter where you are in life, no matter what you think you've accomplished, you have to question how happy your life will actually be. It's not always about money or prestige, but how your inner soul feels when you put your head down on the pillow each night.

In 1980 I started a new career. It began at Northwestern University Dental School, class of 1984. I was a transplant from Brooklyn, NY. This was my first time away from home, my family, and all the friends that I grew up with. To say these were exciting times for me is an understatement. I would wake up, look at Lake Michigan, and wonder how I actually got here. It was like I was living someone else's life and waiting for the next moment of serendipity to occur.

Well, on a random summer night in 1981, it all happened. I was walking down Rush Street with my roommates and glanced at a beautiful young lady through the window of a popular watering hole. Our eyes met, and I kept walking. A chance encounter that happens every day with no further explanation or follow-through. Except that was not the case here. I convinced my buddies to walk back to the bar later in the evening and, to my surprise, my lady was still at the window seat. The four of us walked in and said hello to the four of them. Now remember, I went to Chicago to become a dentist. I was 24 and had a whole life ahead of me to meet a wife, have kids, and build a house with a white picket fence. Well, at least that's what I thought.

Donna and I exchanged phone numbers. Talked forever. Loved going to different restaurants 3-4 times a week. I couldn't believe how all this happened. We were engaged after six weeks, got married eight months later, and then the family began. Jennifer was born in May of 1984. Just a month before my graduation. David was born 18 months later and, after a six-year cooling off period, we had Sarah in 1992.

Life was very hectic. I started a dental practice from scratch in a blue collar, semi-rural town called Joliet. 37 years later I'm still in the same location, treating the same patients and their kids and their kids. In some cases, 5 generations. I'm a big believer that if it's not broke don't fix it. My practice was in cruise control and I was along for the ride.

My son David was playing hockey and I spent most of my free time at hockey rinks. In 1995 I met one of my all-time sports idols at a grand opening of a new ice arena. It was Bobby Hull. For those who aren't familiar with the name Bobby Hull, go to Google university and look him up. You'll see that he is one of the greatest hockey players that ever played the game. He was the first athlete, in any sport, to make a million dollars, establishing the big contracts we see today. He has been a worldwide ambassador loved my so may fans, and he became one of my best friends.

Bobby became part of my family. He was at our house for many Thanksgiving dinners, many family special events, and always knew he had a quiet place to stay when he wanted to get away from all the fanfare and tumult. He would fall asleep on my recliner after telling us great stories about classic games between the Blackhawks and their rival Detroit Redwings. He loved to reminisce and today, at 83, he doesn't miss a detail. When Bobby would fall asleep, I'd witness some very strange behavior in his sleeping pattern. He'd snore very loudly for quite some time, then stop, as if he wasn't breathing. This would be followed up by a loud deep breath and his arousal, and he'd go back to sleep. The snoring would start up again. This would be repeated for hours on end. I did not like what was happening to my friend, and I wanted him to get help. I began my research into obstructive sleep apnea, it's causes, and the different ways it could be treated.

I read all I could find on this condition. I would go to sleep labs and find mentors who were well versed in the field of sleep medicine. Physicians prescribe CPAP machines to help people breathe properly through the night. This therapy works, but the compliance is very low. Not many people like wearing a mask over their face attached to a hose attached to a loud pump. In the dental field, we fabricate a custom-made oral appliance that keeps your lower jaw slightly forward when you go to sleep. The tongue is actually attached to the mandible and it stays forward, keeping it away from the uvula and preventing it from closing off the airway in the back of your throat. I was getting such great results from my patients who had a sleep apnea diagnosis that I wanted to transition my general dentistry practice into more of a sleep medicine clinic.

Unfortunately, my business plans came to a screeching halt. In 2015, my wife Donna became someone I didn't know anymore. Her personality totally changed. She was always confused and simple tasks became a challenge. All my free time was spent taking her to doctors to try and figure out what was wrong with her. Eventually, a special brain scan revealed the answer none of us wanted to hear. She had frontal lobe dementia, a progressive incurable disease that would eventually take her life. She was only 60 years old. Life would never be the same as I became her main caregiver.

2019 proved to be a very rough year. Donna had 4 seizures, each one requiring an ambulance ride to the hospital and a week's stay there. Then in February of 2020, the unthinkable happened. She needed to go to the ER. Donna spent a week in the hospital, then needed to go to a rehab center to get her strength back and coordination. At first, I was able to visit her daily, until the dreaded Corona virus changed all of our lives forever. They put an end to all visitation. A woman with dementia could not see her family, only strangers with masks on. Donna did not understand why she was there, or why she was banished from the family. It was the most horrible thing any family could ever go through. Six weeks of hell that I still cannot get out of my mind.

In May of 2020, as quickly as God put Donna in my life on that Friday evening in 1981, he decided it was time to take her back. She got a fever the first of the month that was diagnosed as Covid-19. Her temperature was 106 on May 6th, and they let me see her on May 7th, the day she passed away. Her room was 411. That happens to be my birthday and Donna's brother's birthday. It was like a message was being sent to me that everything is okay, that she really is in a better place, with her mother and father.

For six months I withdrew into a shell. I felt like my life was over. I had no more purpose or direction, but I just knew that this story I was living had to have a better ending. How could such a charmed life come to such a crashing end? I had to change things up and get back on track. I had so much more living to do. I know my late wife loved watching me dance, sing, making people laugh with my Brooklyn humor, and she'd hate to see me suffer.

One night something compelled me to go online to meet a new companion. With Covid, it seemed like the only way to find that "someone." I met quite a few ladies, but no one really made my heart skip a beat. Until one night, November 2nd, 2020. A total serendipitous moment, round 2. My movie screenplay was writing its ending that very week.

There she was, a beautiful brunette with the greatest smile and a family of four dogs on her lap. Dr. Kim Martin was her name. You'll see her as a contributing author in this book. We went for lunch two days after we spoke and, as they say, the rest is history.

Our love for each other, our doggies, the care we have for those not as fortunate as we are, our morals and values is nothing short of a miracle. When I first asked Kim what music she liked and she said Barry Manilow, I thought it was some kind of joke. You see, I played the piano and sang Barry Manilow music for my late wife when we first met. There are so many commonalities that we have between us that there is not enough space in this chapter to talk about.

Kim has been my inspiration, my life's new compass. She has gotten me back on track with my business plans and then some. I have been trained in Botox therapy, have a new sleep apnea website I'm marketing, and we will be working together in each of our offices. I have a companion to share my joy of watching my 5 grandchildren grow up.

I am a lucky man. I've been through so much in my life, but as long as you're alive and keep an open mind to the plan that the universe has for you, you'll be able to achieve the happiness that you deserve. Seize the opportunities that are presented to you, like I did when I messaged Kim. By now we will be at Bobby Hull's second birthday party together. I'm living life, large and in charge .....Again !!!!!

DR. JEFFRY LAPSKER, DDS

Dr. Jeffry Lapsker has been treating Obstructive Sleep Apnea (OSA) for over seven years. Sleep Well Joliet specializes in treating snoring and sleep apnea. Dr. Lapsker believes in treating his sleep patients as he would his staff or family. He provides all treatment options and discusses the advantages and disadvantages of using an oral appliance to treat sleep apnea. Dr. Lapsker is a graduate of Northwestern Dental School, class of 1984, and an active member of the American Academy of Dental Sleep Medicine (AADSM). He believes in the value of continuing education to advance his level of skill and knowledge with various groups throughout the country. Within walking distance of Sleep Well Joliet, Dr. Lapsker has a unique support system of trusted and experienced ENT Surgical Consultants and a primary care physician that helps him make decisions and help treat the "whole" patient. Sleep Well Joliet has experience working with medical insurance. Dr. Lapsker's staff is trained in getting claims approved for the treatment and getting payments.

Connect with Dr. Lapsker at https://sleepwelljoliet.com.

CHAPTER FOURTEEN

TOMORROW IS ALWAYS FRESH WITH NO MISTAKES IN IT!

by Julie Brown
https://www.facebook.com/julbro

"We are admitting her into the mental health ward at the hospital because she wants to go home and kill herself tonight."

The therapist's words cut through the silence in the room and landed on me with a crushing blow. I could hardly make out the words that followed. I found myself sitting in a circle of mental health experts staring into the black, hollow eyes of someone I barely recognized. I marveled how strange that this was the child I had nurtured every day for more than 18 years, and somehow she looked like a stranger. This twilight zone moment was intensified by a dozen accusing eyes scrutinizing ME.

Minutes later, I raced home to confiscate the weapon! I don't remember how fast I drove to embark on a frantic search to save my daughter from the "villain" in her room. In a frenzy, I rummaged through every drawer. I swiped my arm under her bed and found her hidden journal. I held it by the spine and separated the pages to allow the offending weapon to fall. Nothing. Respect for her privacy wasn't on my radar when I started to read. I hoped to find the answer to the question of "why." She was beautiful, well-loved by everyone, funny, intelligent, talented, and confident. Why would she want to end her own life?

I flipped through the pages searching for clues. Find them, I did. I was stunned to fall upon words that identified me as her enemy, her trigger, and her reason. Fear turned to bitter sorrow. Tears stung my cheeks as they fell. I was stunned, confused, hurt, and heartbroken. I felt helpless and clueless and could not make sense of this revelation. In that journal, I found my new self-proclaimed title, the name I would identify myself as for the next few years.

"Piece of crap mom."

I was the villain. I was a "piece of crap mom" who caused my child to want to end her own life. The fact that I couldn't identify how I failed seemed to validate my guilt.

Finding the blade afterward, seemed insignificant. I was the object of her pain. I was the reason. If I could have died at that moment and she could be happy again, I would have gladly succumbed. I felt lost. That day was a catalyst for the most painful time of my life.

After ten days of treatment, she was released into the care of her best friend's mom. She became the new mom. The one she wanted and needed. As distressing as it was to not be the one to comfort her, I was hopeful the new mom could offer her the kind of nurturing she needed.

I was advised against connecting in any way. My sister urged me to contact her energetically. This was a new concept for me. I was skeptical. Nevertheless, each morning I stood on my back porch to speak to her spirit to spirit. I reached out my arms in the direction of her new home and spoke to her with my whole heart.

"I love you! I'm so sorry if I have hurt you. I hope you feel joy and peace today. I love you sweet daughter."

I hoped that magically she could receive the love that I felt and wanted to give her. Regardless, it helped me to feel like I was doing something. If my neighbors saw my dramatic daily offerings, they might have thought I was crazy!

Days turned into weeks. Weeks into months as she reached out to everyone in the family but me. My role as her protector and caregiver was over. It was me she apparently needed protection from. The separation was excruciating for me personally. In an effort to help in the only way I felt equipped, I prayed and pleaded with God to heal my child. I still feared that I would get a call that she was gone and had given in to the impulse to end her life and it would be my fault! I sunk into depression myself and my happiness seemed to hinge on her happiness or lack thereof.

One day, while reading the Bible, I came across a powerful story I knew well. I read how Jesus faced the greatest trial of His earthly mission and fasted for forty days and forty nights. I paused. Could I do this? If I did, would God recognize my extraordinary faith and heal my daughter and our relationship – or would I die? Would it even matter?

I discovered on the internet while researching that someone had done this and actually lived to tell of their experience. I decided to face the harrowing challenge, hoping that this act of extreme faith would bring healing and forgiveness. I wanted to have her back in my life, and I also wanted to feel whole again.

Day 1, 2, 3… it was going to be harder than I thought. 7, 8, 9… although I was growing weak, I was determined to offer this sacrifice. Day 14, 15, 16… I felt like the walking dead. I felt empty and powerless. My heart ached with grief. At three weeks, my husband begged me to stop. I assured him I would quit if I detected any signs I could die. I went on drinking only water, not a morsel of food and, by this point, spending most of my time in bed or on the couch. My prayers were fervent, and I resolved to finish. If this was the way to save my daughter and get her back in my life, it was a small price to pay.

I stood in the shower on day 30 letting the warm water run down my face and without warning, everything went black. Next thing I remember, I found myself on the tile floor looking up at the spray of water coming down all around me. I felt a throbbing pain on the side of my head. I must have hit it when I collapsed. My shoulder was sore and already bruised. I lay there wondering if I could find the strength to get up on my own. I pushed myself up to a sitting position and did some contemplation. After a while, I willed myself to stand. I grabbed a towel and stumbled my way to the bed where I could recover and rest.

I kept my promise to my husband. Although I secretly hadn't cared if I lived or died, I had promised I would quit if I thought I could die. Passing out and hitting my head was a sign that could happen. As the person who was crowned "piece of crap mom," I thought I deserved to die. When faced with my own mortality, though, I realized I wanted to live. I ended my fast on day thirty with some vegetable juice. I prayed my exercise in faith would be enough to warrant the miracles I was seeking. I didn't make it to forty days, but I tried my best. I spent the next week in the painful process of reintroducing food slowly into my system as my digestive track was no longer working correctly.

In the end, I didn't see the miracle I prayed for. I saw only more evidence of the distance between us and a lack of healing. I realized that not even God would intervene when it interfered with someone's will. However, that moment I found myself in a crumpled heap on the shower floor changed everything.

The miracle would not be what I prayed for, yet God did answer my prayer in His own way.

I wanted to live!

I wanted a way out of the grief that had for so long followed me like a dark cloud. I wanted to feel the joy of waking up in the morning, excited for a new day. I desperately wanted to *really* live again. This desire seemed to be in opposition to what I felt I deserved. Honestly, I wasn't sure how to let go of the pain and grief. I wore it like a badge of shame on my chest.

I wanted to stop feeling sad. No amount of reassurance I got from my other children seemed to matter. That label, "piece of crap mom," persisted in my mind. I punished myself so hard for not being what she needed, it haunted me. I knew I needed to finally let it go. With difficulty, I chose a new mantra.

"I am an amazing mom who is exactly what my children need."

This needed to be MY truth. Over and over, I whispered what I wanted to be, trying to feel it inside. Letting go of my self-defeating beliefs about myself would take time. However, deep down, I knew my worth was not dependent on what someone else thought of me. I couldn't control someone's perceptions about me. The truth was deep in my heart. I loved deeply and earnestly. I worked hard to be the best mom I could be. And choosing a new path for my own wellness is how I eventually won my personal battle.

There's no going back. No one can change the past. Making peace with myself meant forgiving myself for not being enough, making mistakes, and behaving badly at times. I gave myself grace. I felt the need to suffer, and I did. Although I had never set out to become a victim, I had become a victim of what others believed about me. I had never considered the value in being kind to myself. I realized that living in the past, and doubting my worth, robbed my future self of the joy and happiness that I longed for. Perhaps some sense had been knocked into me, under the raining faucet in the shower!

I felt inspired to reread my favorite book my mother had read to our family at the breakfast table when we were children. *Anne of Green Gables* was about a goodhearted orphan who always was getting herself into trouble. Her story shook me out of my pattern of self-defeating thoughts. This young girl was filled with imagination and saw the world with wonderment and awe. She taught me to embrace optimism and hope. Hope was exactly what I needed at that moment. I focused on her mantra, "Tomorrow is always fresh with no mistakes in it."

Peace filled my soul as I read these words over and over. Tomorrow could be whatever I wanted it to be. Her mantra is a true definition of hope and it became mine, too.

My life took on a new purpose. I spent my time in service, sharing love, and learning. It was time to fulfill my lifelong dream of learning to play the piano. Music helped more than I can put into words. Music heals, but making my own music delighted me and created a new sense of accomplishment. Even though I hit as many wrong notes as right ones, it brought me a new feeling of joy.

My friend encouraged me to find a way to serve others. I started going to the local food bank with her to hand out food to the needy. I met wonderful people and my world grew richer with those relationships.

I did discover happiness on the other side of sorrow. I found it was in my power all along to create it. I just needed to choose it! I needed to be the creator of my own joyful reality. Glenda the Good Witch had it right, "You had the power all along, my dear!"

And yes… my daughter eventually came around. Our story is still evolving, but I continue to believe tomorrow is fresh and filled with wonderful possibilities (and no mistakes!).

JULIE BROWN

Julie Brown, author, speaker, and recruiter at hubTEN Global is passionate about making the world a better place by collaborating on many projects to bring people together to share their gifts. The world is a better place when good people inspire and create together.

The grateful mom of five terrific grown children, the happy wife of the handsome Kirk Brown, and grandma to the five cutest kids on earth, home is where Julie hangs her heart! When she isn't orchestrating family fun, she may be practicing the piano or volunteering at the local food bank. She feels called to head up personal history projects to help her loved ones become unforgettable. She has helped publish three histories and is currently working on two more. In years past, she was a professional dancer, choreographer, and studio owner. She is now content to attend productions as an enthusiastic audience member. Julie's entrepreneurial spirit is satisfied in her leadership in doTERRA and sharing natural solutions to heal the mind and body. Helping others create wealth and healing has brought her much joy. Julie and her family reside in the beautiful state of Utah where they relish having four seasons.

Connect with Julie here https://www.facebook.com/julbro.

CHAPTER FIFTEEN

DENIAL ALMOST KILLED ME

by Julie Donelson
Founder & Creator, Julie Donelson Brands, LLC
www.JulieDonelson.com

I went to bed that night hiding a secret from my family.

It was late summer in Illinois. I lived with my junior high school aged kids and husband in a small older home we had vowed to renovate, but never did. I had some months prior been diagnosed with high blood pressure and was put on medication to help control it. I was not thrilled with being on meds, particularly since in my early 40s I felt I was 'too young' to be needing such a thing. I had an extremely stressful job. I was very active doing all the things I could for my kids, their schools, and activities (scouting, swim team, music programs, etc.) I was also active in my own clubs, organizations, church. To say I had taken on WAY too many things is an understatement. I only came to recognize some years into my wellness journey that this was a common phenomenon, creating "busy" to take attention off of the pain/stress/etc. I was in, so I didn't have to deal with it.

Quick note - that shit doesn't work.

I had come home that afternoon from the hospital. I didn't tell my husband I even had an appointment with the doctor, let alone ended up in the hospital clinic. I had strange heart palpitations or something odd that had happened a couple of times and a call to my doctor led to a referral for an EKG and a request to wear a heart monitor for 24 hours. So, here I was, coming home on a Friday evening, wearing a heart monitor under my clothes, never even breathing a word of it to anyone in my family, not a friend, neighbor or anyone. I kept the entire thing a secret.

Was I being brave or was I in denial? Denial. But that would soon change, thankfully. Everyone has their moment of truth. The moment when things cross a line, or hit rock bottom, or however you think of it. This was one of my moments. It was actually one event in a small series of events that changed me. Had I been paying closer attention, maybe one of the events would have been enough. But I suppose you could call me stubborn. I just kept on with living the same way, until there I was. Trying to keep a heart monitor and all the accompanying wires hidden from my family for 24 hours and going to bed thinking to myself that if I really did end up with a significant heart problem, would I even wake up tomorrow? What if I didn't? Then what? What about my kids who I did so much for? Who I loved like I wanted to love myself?

Let me be honest, I had never once considered my own mortality up until that night. I was in life threatening situations almost daily, my job as a child protection worker sent me into some sketchy situations. I never once feared for my own safety. Never once in the thousands of hours I spent driving all over my state, in all types of horrific weather, and transporting clients alone in my mom minivan had I felt in any danger. Again, bravery or just denial? Hm. Seems like that keeps coming up.

At the time, I was barely surviving life, and the fact that something may just take me down out of nowhere was the wake-up moment I desperately needed. Did my life change dramatically that following morning when I did wake up? No. However, I was able to begin that day to make changes. Long-lasting changes that now have me thriving in my life, instead of just surviving and getting by on sheer force of will.

Since that time over 15 years ago, I've learned I am far from alone in this situation. In fact, many of the women I work with now come to me after recognizing in themselves the survival mode they've been in is not helping them achieve the life they really want. Sure, survival is important, but after that, there are many richer and more meaningful levels to life that are waiting for you, that you CAN have. And frankly, they aren't nearly as hard to get to as we think. Survival to vitality is only a few small steps away.

Prior to that 24-heart monitor, I had been existing on coffee, Diet Mt. Dew, sugar, carbs, stubbornness, junk food, and force of will. I didn't eat real meals, and when I did they were far from healthy. I had high blood pressure, was nearly 300 pounds, had chronic migraines, and never-ending back pain. None of this would really be a surprise to anyone, but again, you just work hard to get through each day and then fall into bed, so you quit noticing things. You just live with it, and move on. Ignoring the compound effects of those actions.

The beauty of the compound effect is that it works both ways, for good and bad. The real assignment then is to turn that compound effect around and begin to steer it in the direction YOU CHOOSE. We've all heard that one salad won't have much impact on a person's overall health in a visible way, but what about a salad a day? For 30 days? Or 90 days? Will THAT have an impact? Heck YES! But here's the problem, we want to see it working or feel it working or us immediately. And just like a bank account with compounding interest, you have to let it build and stick with it before you notice the results are happening.

The book, The Compound Effect by Darren Hardy, is one of my favorite books to recommend to my clients when they start off on their own health, wellness, fitness, or life changing journey. It's a quick read, but powerfully demonstrates how all the small actions work in ways that are almost imperceptible until BAM!, the tipping point happens.

Most times, when we have a goal or vision of what we want for our life, we see the dream result but not the steps that fill in the gap from where we are to where we want to be. This is my specialty and what I LOVE helping women with filling in!

For example, in my own situation, I was so far from a vibrantly healthy, wealthy person, I couldn't see how it was possible to get where I wanted to be. Did I mention I was in debt for well into 5 figures as well? Yeah, that too. Survival mode and denial. Sigh.

At the time, after I returned that heart monitor and later got the result, an all clear and change of medication I was apparently reacting to, I knew I could no longer live how I was living and I needed to do something, anything to move me toward a better place. So, it began. For no particular reason, I decided to start with giving up the beloved Diet Mt. Dew. The beautiful tasty drink I had with me 24 hours a day. By my bed at night, in the car, on my desk, hot or cold, flat or bubbly. I would drink it all day, every day. I can't recall why I chose that particular thing to change, but I was spending a LOT of money buying it, and planned car trips around where I could stop and get more of it, from a fountain (my favorite way to have it). Sounds like an addict's behavior, doesn't it? It may be legal, but is it any better than any other addiction? Nope.

I have since learned there are many things we can become addicted to, and addictions themselves are at first just behaviors that become patterns, that then morph and change our thinking, finally becoming so entrenched we don't even notice them. By the time they become entrenched, it's difficult (but not impossible) to undo.

The real message I want to give you is that all the secrets you keep, the fears, the secret dreams for your life that seem so crazy to speak out loud, even to your best friend, are all things you have the power to change in any way you like. You may think you've got something that you 'can't change,' but I challenge you to think about the parts of it you can change. Even someone with say Type 1 Diabetes who MUST have medication can certainly change their eating habits, improve their diet to better support their health and body functions. A person with thyroid issues CAN eat and supplement in a way that supports good thyroid function, and will lead to better health overall. Just because you have (insert your health, medical, etc. reason here) doesn't mean you are POWERLESS OVER IT to some degree. I want you to begin to question your own self on what you've been surviving and find out if there is a small way you can add or subtract from your behaviors/actions that can lead to an improvement of that condition in some way.

And yes, I am aware that some conditions cannot be changed.

But let me be totally blunt. Most of us are just making excuses. The majority of us CAN CHANGE things, at least to a degree. And wouldn't it be better to feel the power of doing something rather than the powerlessness of staying stuck where you are right now?

My own wellness came in increments, but I've long since kicked the Diet Mt. Dew addiction. I have no more chronic migraines, haven't had one in over a decade. I have been off high blood pressure meds. I lost weight. I was able to train for and complete 5ks, 10ks and half marathons. I started biking, did some 'sprint' triathlons, earned my open water scuba certification, climbed Mt. Kilimanjaro, zip-lined, rappelled down a mountain and a waterfall (SO FUN), and done some other very cool things that back on that day in late summer I was wearing that heart monitor I couldn't even have dreamed of doing. All I wanted was to FEEL BETTER.

My journey to better overall wellness will never end. It's a place to live in, not just a destination you reach and stop. It's something I do every day, habits I've built into my routine. Daily gratitude, daily intentions, daily quiet time, daily seeking what I want and not allowing myself to be sucked into or manipulated by drama or outside forces seeking to spread their negativity onto someone else. Self-care and wellness is not just weight or fitness, it's physical, mental, spiritual, emotional, financial, and relationships.

That's your magic start, my friend. Just something small that will help you feel better.

Less TV

Less stress

Less "news"

Less junk food

Less making excuses

Less giving up on yourself

Less drama in relationships

Less worrying what others think

Less burning the candle at both ends

Less hanging around negative people

More moving your body, even it's just marching in place

More finding hobbies that engage your brain

More time with people who lift you up

More things to make you laugh

More days enjoying nature

More trying new things

More playfulness

More meditation

More gratitude

More dancing

More veggies

More water

More walks

More sleep

JULIE DONELSON

Julie Donelson is a social worker of over 30 years turned wellness coach, writer, and product creator. She loves helping women close the gap from where they are to where they want to be.

You can connect with Julie here https://juliedonelson.com.

CHAPTER SIXTEEN

MY HYBRID HEALING WELLNESS JOURNEY

by Katia N. Miller Pagan
Physician and Founder, K Miller Wellness Clinic
www.facebook.com/KMillerWellness

I thought I had it all figured out by my Senior Year of Internal Medicine: a sub-specialty in a teaching hospital, followed by administrative duties, and then leadership roles. By spring 2015, things were not looking so great. I woke up with a weird, burning, painful sensation in my right mid-lower chest area. Remembering my strenuous workout the day before, I gave it no attention. As a natural klutz, I then ignored my subtle trips with my right foot while on high heels and didn't make a connection. I later noticed that this area also felt numb to water and to my own touch. I thought, *'Ufff, this has to be Shingles. Let's ask an attending about it tomorrow, it's definitely stress.'*

The next day, walking to the hospital, I was stumbling on flats and found it weird. *'Shingles, doesn't do this. This can't be happening.'*

I spoke to my Chief Resident, then my Program Director, and was quickly sent to the Neurology Department. When the neurologist asked me to raise my right knee against his hand strength and resistance and couldn't, I was officially scared. I was sent off to an MRI, missing my day's work and a job interview. *'What is happening? I'm a doctor, I work out, I am healthy, What is this?'*

That night at my scheduled shift, unsuccessfully attempting to ignore the burning, painful sensation in my right side, my mind kept racing. *'What is this? What is wrong with me? Why now?'*

The following day, I headed back to my Neurologist, in denial after reading "… lesions consistent with a Demyelinating Disease." My Program Director read my results, gave me a diagnosis, and after reassuring me he knows the best specialists, sent me to a nearby hospital. I was admitted for intravenous medications. *'This can't be happening.'*

For five days, I had never had that much alone time in my own head. I thought justice and redemption would release me from resentment and chose to acquire more titles, more degrees, and more money. Back then, I had no personal power to radically accept that my results, my health, my outcomes were mine to own and heal. I thought it should be financial stability first to then allow myself the freedom to honor my body. In the meantime, I did what I could with food, working out, and resting. *'This hospital thing won't stop me.'*

Eating healthy was a challenge. I had no time or resources. It was expensive to buy and it would take forever to grow. Working out, another challenge, inconsistent work schedule and the patient victim mindset. Resting well, even more challenging. I found myself requiring a physician for prescribed medications in exchange for a few hours of consistent rest. *'When I get money, I will have more time for healthier habits.'*

Then another 'event' in my right ear. I lost auditory acuity and raising the volume or loud noise made everything painful. Taking the oral version of medications, further 'confirmed' my 'diagnosis.' I knew my desire for money had me exchanging time for money, with two jobs and no rest or recovery. I thought this would solve the money problem. *'After all, the specialist said we get to wait and see as clinical evidence is still inconclusive.'*

The third 'event' got my left hand. Unable to fully feel or move my hand was limiting. I forced my hand to write, only calling my doctor when writing became too painful for the other muscles. *'I can't work like this. Way to be the example, Doctor.'*

I was told I had to be admitted and somehow convinced my doctor to treat me at home by sending an infusion company for the intravenous medication. I was then told, "I believe it's time you consider treatment." There I was, for five more days, unaware my body was asking me to slow down. *'I need treatment? Maldita sea!'*

I read literature from intravenous, to injections, to pills, and had conversations about side effects on myself or if pregnant. Dreading the liver and kidney function routinely monitoring as well as lymphocytes and bone marrow, in absolute denial. *'I finish Internal Medicine, a patient? What kind of an oxymoron is this? A Doctor Patient. How Embarrassing!'*

Of course, I felt called to eat, rest, and be healthy and had no resources. Afraid of another 'event,' I gave in to the pill summer of 2016 and began the physical struggle with the side effects, the stomach pain, nausea and diarrhea, and the skin flushing. Then the mental struggle with the pill for the condition, the pill for the stomach, and then the pill to sleep all while trying to keep up with life. Then the disempowering struggle with the health insurance and their rules about expensive pills. *'Fully employed, great salary, and still required to pay extra monthly? Compliance is not as easy as it looks.'*

I felt like a sad karmic story as everything changed for the worse. Initially I thought relocating my family would bring more opportunities, and finishing as a half broke, sub-specialist with bad credit and an autoimmune disease as the icing on the cake was not what I had in mind. I felt shame now, so I buried myself more into work. *'Focus on vacations, at least there's still that.'*

Winter 2016, I experienced my first awakening. Reconnecting with nature away from home, deep in the cold snowy mountains, I found blissful freedom. I knew I wasn't happy with my career path, and returned to it, as it was the only thing I knew. *'You know, we got bills to pay.'*

Summer 2017 was my second awakening. Away in nature, exposed to its healing power, I knew the pills were not the way and chose to stop them. I still worked hard buried in shame and guilt feeling my past medical history lingering like a shadow. I kept from pursuing new academic opportunities resentful for the safe job. In spite of no 'events' as of spring 2016 and no medications as of summer 2017, it was lather, rinse, repeat. *'Safe job, stable health insurance, just in case.'*

Spring 2019, my third awakening. Amazed with how nature's colorful essence brought so much peace to my soul. After juggling 80-hour work-weeks, I knew I wanted to be my own boss and also bring forth health. That summer, I began research in alternative medicine. Western medicine and outpatient clinics, currently overwhelmed physicians with approximately 20+ patients in one day, averaging 15-30 minutes with each patient. I held a strong belief that patients with several chronic conditions, over 10 daily prescribed medications, required more than 15 minutes' time and constantly lost the battle to awareness of mindset and lifestyle habits to the pills for every ill perspective. *'If I only had the time to show them.'*

December 2019 was my fourth awakening. On a cold, snowy mountaintop, with the sun rays hitting the mountaintops, overlooking trees and the houses in the valley with the smoke in the chimneys drifting in the wind, and the cold snowflakes on my face I found blissful peace. I noticed nature made my mind slow down. In the stillness, there were no sacrifices, struggles, stressors or suffering and felt driven to focus on creating more opportunities like this. A prayer was born within my soul as snowflakes fell on my cheeks.

> *"Work hard for what you want. Stay focused on your goals. Respect your body. Respect your mind. Listen and honor yourself always. Humble your spirit and soul. Be grateful for what you already have. May 2020's blessings be as plentiful as snowflakes."*

Not knowing how to make it all come to pass, I began my journey back to my steady 40-hour workweek and was invited to participate in a 21 Day Detoxify Your Mind Program. It stimulated my awareness into thought patterns that drove me into action. A Six Week Shred Challenge was next and I combined high intensity interval training with intermittent fasting and a ketogenic diet. I enjoyed learning and creating more fun and tasty ways to eat and stay healthy. I wanted to use my medical knowledge and combine it to what I was learning about alternative medicine and provide the freedom to empower wellness in everyone. *'If I could open my private practice? Nah, it wouldn't work.'*

They say when the student is ready the master appears. As I practiced meditation enabling my mind, exercised daily, and ate healthier enabling my body, I was slowly enabling my soul to understand the true purpose of my calling. I learned about how domesticated familiar habits, patterns, and unknown daily environmental exposures can lead us into inflammation, chronic disease, and cancer. I met Healers that had already made the body mind connection to the reversal of medical conditions such as cancer through meditation, healing, and mindful awareness and felt called to study more about the power of the body and mind. Then began making the connection of the gut on the body and the mind. *'My concept is unconventional. What if I open a Wellness Center?'*

As everyone started noticing my changes, I began opening up to my clients, patients, and colleagues that asked and that got them inspired. I spoke about intermittent fasting with several dietary changes, high intermittent interval training, and meditation. Those who applied what resonated started noticing changes and they were inspired to continue. In the follow-up visits, I was removing instead of adding pills. As some no longer required anti-anxiety or sleeping pills, others required less medications for hypertension and cholesterol lowering drugs or insulin after losing weight. I knew I had too much evidence to ignore. The power of the mind and the power of choice was key. Waiting for the diagnosis, or the pill as I did, is one way. The other is the choice to honor your mind, body, and soul. When I chose to listen to my mind and honor my body, I gave my soul blissful freedom.

The following things created a mindful awareness in my own inner mind, body and soul journey to wellness.

To nurture my mind, I tune in to thoughts and feelings. If I notice emotions of fear, anger, jealousy, revenge, hatred, superstition, greed or envy, if away from nature, I find a mental image I can hold for 90 seconds or more. I remember I'm there as I relax every muscle of my body as I inhale and exhale deeply. I find that emotion, thought or that part of my body that requires attention. I use music or free writing until I can find emotions of compassion, peace, and love. I use personal development and that focuses on leadership and emotional intelligence. *'My outside is a mirror of my inside.'*

To nurture my body, I move and breathe. I dance or exercise at least 12-25 minutes of my day. It varies according to how I feel. When it comes to food, I consider what's closest to me in season, in its fresh and purest state. I cook my vegetables, use healthy sugar substitutes, combine spices that support digestion, absorption and elimination according to my body type. I love combining infusions, my favorite detox infusion is coriander, cumin and fennel seeds, CCF tea. I love learning new ways Ayurveda can be part of my Hybrid Healing Practice. *'I am what I eat and what I don't eliminate.'*

To nurture my soul, I enjoy grounding in nature and meditation. I fill my home with inspiring music, candle scents and flowers. I sing or dance, connect with animals and embrace things that give me chills. *'I am called to embrace and express my purpose.'*

When I chose to honor and listen to my body, everything fell into place. I now believe I am here as evidence outside of the pill for every ill perspective. It's 2021, and the follow-up MRI no longer shows active demyelinating lesions in my mid chest area. *'The Doctor Patient, Embodied Hybrid Healing Wellness Journey.'*

KATIA N MILLER PAGAN

Katia N Miller Pagan is a Puerto Rican physician who was diagnosed with an autoimmune disease, which led to her dedicating her time to learn more about the healing power of the mind and conscious medicine through proper foods that honor the body's unique composition. Her desire is to open a Hybrid Healing Wellness Retreat Center that can be of support to those on their own Wellness Journey.

You can connect with Katia here:
https://facebook.com/KMillerWellness.

CHAPTER SEVENTEEN

SEVEN MINUTES THAT TRANSFORMED MY LIFE

by Dr. Katrina Esau
President & CEO, KE3 Worldwide Enterprises
www.drkatrinaesau.com

One of the greatest things that I had always wanted to do prior to me receiving salvation was to read the word of God in its entirety. But every time I tried, I was distracted by confusion. Every time I arrived at the point where it was explaining the Biblical lineage of historical families (i.e. Ner begat Kish, Kish begat Saul, Saul begat Jonathan, and so on) I was perplexed. No one had ever told me it wasn't a good idea to start at Genesis as a babe in Christ, so I was hindered in accomplishing my desire. One day, while attending a prayer brunch, I was given a handout titled, *7 Minutes With God - You Can Receive Christ Now by Faith Through Prayer (Prayer is Talking with God)*. Needless to say, it got my attention. It clearly described how to spend that seven minutes and starting in Genesis was not it! I eagerly put it into practice daily and found that seven minutes ultimately turned into hours. While you may not have hours to spend in His presence, surely you have seven minutes.

Those seven minutes were the best part of my day and it gave me a spiritual foundation that I didn't know I would later need as I walked through the most tumultuous season of my life, separation from my husband as a result of infidelity. Had I not had that time to build the most important relationship of my life, I wouldn't be in a place today where I'm able to help other women heal from the pain of infidelity. I could have very well been in prison, an insane asylum, on drugs, or any number of things—BUT GOD. He had a different plan for my life. He covered me and kept me so that I would be able to help other women walk through their journey of healing.

As such, I believe it is important to have a solid spiritual foundation and build a relationship with God. Having a relationship and knowing His word will sustain you and carry you through the journey of life. We all have trials and tribulations we will encounter and having a solid foundation is what will help us to not give up. It was my relationship with God that kept me in the midst of depression, anger, shame, and guilt. Without Him, there truly would be no me. Knowing how to pray and having a relationship with God showed me who I am. It allowed me to see myself the way God sees me. It allowed me to take authority over my life and cast down the word curses and generational curses that were over me and my bloodline. It helped me to forgive my husband and love him unconditionally. It was through my relationship with God that I learned how to love me. I learned how to take care of me and embrace who God created me to be. It changed my speech and transformed my mind. It showed me the importance of rebuilding trust and how to go about doing it.

It is important to read the word of God daily. Getting to know Him will bring healing, deliverance, and peace. It will transform your life in many ways. The word of God is a mirror, and it will reveal the truth and promises God has spoken over your life. It will also uncover the lies spoken to you and over you so you can denounce them and walk in freedom. God loves us and is concerned about every area of our lives. He draws nigh to those that draw nigh to him. It's His word that gives us direction and insight.

Are you ready to transform your mind? Your life? Your family? Here is the breakdown of the seven minutes.

REMEMBER: Do this daily. Pick a specific time of day and commit to it.

First 30 seconds: prepare your heart.

For me, this was communicating my gratitude and asking God to remove anything from my heart that would hinder my ability to hear from Him or prevent Him from hearing me. I would ask Him to write His word on the tablet of my heart that I might not sin against Him.

Next four minutes: read the bible.

Start with the Gospels beginning with the Book of Mark. It's recommended not to stop and do a Word study but, instead, to just read consecutively verse after verse, chapter after chapter. After Mark, go to John, and so on. This was sometimes a challenge for me because it is hard for me to move on without understanding, hence the reason my seven minutes would continue to grow.

After God has spoken through the reading of His word, it is time to speak back to Him in prayer.

The last two and half minutes: fellowship with God in four areas referred to as ACTS – Adoration, Confession, Thanksgiving, Supplication.

Start today and your life will never be the same. If you feel like you need a starting prayer, here's what one may look like:

> *Lord, you are holy. There is none like you. You are the I AM, the rose of Sharon, the lily in the field, my bright and morning star. You are the lifter of my head and the lover of my soul. Thank you, Jesus, for yet another day and another opportunity to get it right with you. Search my heart O God and remove anything that is not like you. Forgive me of my sin and trespasses. Thank you for being a merciful and just God. Thank you for my life, health, and strength. Thank you, Lord, for active use of my limbs, for the roof over my head, transportation, a job to go to,*

food on my table. Thank you for my family. Thank you for keeping us as we slumbered and slept. Glory to your name God. Lord, go before me this day and make crooked places straight. I dispatch the angels assigned to my life to go before me and gather the harvest with my name on it. No weapon formed against me or my family shall prosper. Lord, put my name in the wind. I thank you for favor with those in positions of authority. Give me eyes to see the doors you have opened before me and the strength and courage to walk boldly through them. I press toward the mark of the higher calling. Thank you, Jesus, for answered prayer. I decree and declare wholeness over every area of my life and according to Job 22:28, it is established. I ask these and all things in Jesus' name, amen.

That is an example of something I would pray. As you spend time with the Lord and learning His words, you will be equipped with scriptures and promises to pray over you and your family.

Prayer is simply communication between you and God. It doesn't have to be complicated or eloquent. He meets us right where we are, and He speaks every language. There are no barriers in prayer. It travels at the speed of light. So, don't hold back, make your requests made known unto Him. It's the promise and privilege He has given to us. As you do so, it will be important to be more aware and sensitive to your words as they have power. You don't want to speak against the very thing you have prayed and are believing God for as it defeats the purpose. Many times, we say things out of habit not realizing the power in our words. They create our atmospheres. When we honestly believe our words have power, it will cause us to be more aware and in tune with what we are saying. It will change our language. Now, with all things people can go to the extreme. For example, it's raining out and you say it is sunny and beautiful. That is exact and may be considered weird opposed to spiritually sound. A more proper use of words in this scenario could be, Lord, thank you for the rain. As it pours so shall the blessings of the Lord over my life. Or perhaps, you want to ask the Lord to stop the rain. Or, simply say nothing. Again, the goal here is not to make it complicated or so spiritually deep that you are no earthly good. Because of my faith, there are times when I would ask, "Lord, please lift your rain long enough for me to make it into the store, house, or wherever." Sometimes He does, other times He doesn't. You never know if you don't ask. Let me take a pause here and just speak a little deeper about the power of your words and speaking negative over you, others, or in general. We've often heard the saying, "sticks and stones may break my ones, but words will never hurt." I have learned this is not the truth.

Negative words leave lasting scars. They have a way of creating a movie reel that stays on repeat and brings lasting damage that produces bad fruit in multiple areas of your life. Many people have heard negative words spoken over them all their life – you'll never be anything, you're only good for this or that, nobody wants you, you're ugly, you're too dark, you're too thin, you're dumb, and the list goes on. As a result, they repeat these words over and over and it builds paradigms that serve as the platform of how they navigate through life. Some would say I don't speak negative over myself, but their actions say something different. Some turn to alcohol, others to drugs, others to abusive men that reinforce the same negative words. It would behoove you to work hard to stop using negative language as it will transform your life. It's one thing for others to speak negative over you, but what you say to yourself matters most. Life and death is in the power of your tongue, so why not create your life, your world beautifully? Use your words to cancel the negative words spoken over you by others including YOURSELF. Stop using negative words to come in agreement with the enemy of your soul. You can do all things through Christ who strengthens you. You are beautiful. You are loved. It may take some time before you start to believe the words you are saying but keep doing it until they take root, and you believe what you are saying.

Negative words have the power to manifest as illness in your body. For example, when you constantly say I'm sick and tired of this, I don't feel well, my head is killing me, etc. These may be true statements, but you can turn them into positive confessions—I am healed. I speak life over my body. Exchanging negative dialogue for positive dialogue will shift your perspective. It will cause the heaviness you may be experiencing to lift. When we focus on positivity, it brings joy.

In summary, making time to build a relationship with God, learning His word, practicing communing with Him, and guarding your words will transform your life. This behavior will bring wellness to many areas of your life, improve your self-love, improve your relationships across the board, and position you to always stand from a posture of victory. Everything I do stems from my relationship with the Lord. As the word says, in Him I move and have my being. He truly is the lifter of my head and the lover of my soul. I pray you've been blessed by the words in this chapter. I pray you will begin to build a relationship or strengthen the one you already have with God. I also speak peace and blessings over you and your family.

DR. KATRINA ESAU

Dr. Katrina Esau is the President and CEO of KE3 Worldwide Enterprises, LLC, the founder of W.H.O.L.E. (Wives Healing Openly Leaving Him Exalted)™, and the creator of The W.H.O.L.E. Academy, which offers programming that cultivates healing and forgiveness. Her ministry was birthed after coming face to face with infidelity in her own marriage, having bouts of hopelessness, and feeling alone in her marital journey. Her mission in life is to help other women hurting from the pain of infidelity reclaim their power and walk in total healing. Dr. Esau is known for her unique style of delivery and coaching that has a way of reaching people where they are and empowering them to come up higher.

Dr. Esau is also a best-selling author of *The Pain of Infidelity Births Purpose* where she shares her story and experience with other women in a real, raw, and relatable way to bring hope, encouragement, and healing to them whether they are entering in, in the midst of, or they walked away from a season of trauma in their marriage. *The Blueprint to Becoming Whole* is the accompanying journal with activities, affirmations, and encouragement. She is a co-author of *Called to Intercede: Volume One*, where she shares on the topic of A Divine Gap Stander.

You can connect with Dr. Katrina here: https://drkatrinaesau.com.

CHAPTER EIGHTEEN

THANK YOU

by Dr. Kim Martin, DC
Founder & Clinical Director,
North Shore Health Solutions
www.NorthShoreHealthSolutions.com

My wellness journey is a mental experience which affects my emotional and physical well-being.

"Thank you" are two words that can have a positive and a negative connotation (depending on the circumstances that you use this expression). As we go through life, we have visions of how we want things to be, then there are unexpected things that happen and we are blindsided, totally taken by surprise. We look at those downtimes as devastating. It is a temporary stage, I promise! I know because I have been there more than once.

Sometimes life doesn't go exactly as we plan. You push the reset button. When you fall six times, make sure you get up seven!! That's my motto!

Because things don't always happen as quickly as we want them to, sometimes we tend to blame and question ourselves. Why did this happen to me? How come it seems so easy for other people? We create negative self-talk. Sometimes we need to get the negativity out of our heads. We have over 60,000 thoughts per day and only about 500 of them are new thoughts. 80% of those thoughts are negative. If your thoughts create emotions and your emotions create actions, then your actions create reality.

Contemplate about what you are thinking daily. If you are thinking the same negative thoughts every day, what are the chances of changing your reality? Isn't that the definition of insanity? But this can be helped by first recognizing that there is an issue. You cannot change what you do not see as a problem. We need to break these negative patterns. Change your thoughts to change your life. One of my favorite things to do at least once per year is to create a decision board. I do not call it a vision board because I don't want to "wish" for things I want to accomplish. I want it to be my DECISION of what I will achieve. That creates a shift in my thinking and gives me my internal motivation to believe and then achieve.

I have always wanted to be a doctor. I wanted to treat people naturally without pharmaceutical drugs. I earned my Doctor of Chiropractic Degree in 1996. I started private practice in 1997.

As part of being a doctor, we become confidants, healers, and friends with our patients. I had visions of a customized program for each patient. I was told by many colleagues that we didn't have enough time to talk to patients, especially if you are a provider with any insurance company. Some insurance companies stressed a limit of eight minutes per patient. That made no sense to me as I had heard for years that your patients will tell you 80% of the diagnosis if you just listen and take a good history. I feel very blessed to have created the type of practice that I would want to go to if I were a patient.

I started my practice in an office share model. Two groundbreaking visionaries that I had the pleasure of knowing were Dr. Rolla Pennell and Dr. Richard Yennie. They taught me how to grow my practice and I was thankful I had the opportunity to be around them, their employees, and families.

It is such a pleasure to see someone with a health issue and you can give them a better quality of life for years to come.

I remember my first week in practice. I had several new patient exams scheduled. I was ready to help anybody with a spine. My son was 13 months old and he had a low-grade fever and was teething. I had to bring him to my office because daycare didn't want him if he had a fever. I took one of my new patients into the exam/Xray room. My son was upset, and we heard his cries in the other room. She told me to let my son come in the room with us. She then said, "Thank You" for seeing her and for being a mom first. My heart was happy, and my gut is shocked. She sat patiently while I gave my son some treatment, then I proceeded to take her health history with the three of us in the room. She had a low back surgery scheduled and was looking for an option to eliminate her pain medications until her surgery. I was excited to be able to examine, develop a treatment protocol, and then treat her. My judgment call had a happy ending as I was able to help her avoid the low back surgery altogether. She was a patient with different health issues and became a friend for many years. She trusted my experience and expertise. We both had the same goals for her health journey. Her success boosted my confidence as a healthcare provider. I learned to say "Thank You" to all those who came before me and my patients that appreciated the help I gave them. She taught me to be empathetic. Since I moved out of state, we still have occasional communication with updates about my son who is now 24 years old.

One of my best friends and patient, Lynn, allowed me to care for her when she lived near me. She moved back to Atlanta to be with her family and start a new career. She had a dream and vision to walk the 2,190 miles along the Appalachian Trail. She would post weekly photos and write about her experiences along the trails. We had figured out how to get her the nutrition she needed each month sent to a hotel because she was limited to 30 pounds on her back which included her tent, clothes, and personal belongings. I was living her dream with her. I loved that she was happy and in her element. I would have been good for about one week of walking. About 600 miles into her journey, she injured her back and flew back to Atlanta to heal before she would be able to go back out and complete her task. I listened to her signs and symptoms and advised her what I would do and the type of doctor she needed to see. I was able to co-treat with her stool and bloodwork results, but I needed her to do physical treatment to speed up the healing process. She said "Thank You" to me all the time. She is back to 100%. I say "Thank You" to her for listening and following through with her treatment plan.

I have another favorite patient of mine. She is a brilliant businesswoman, mother, jazz singer, actress, patient, and friend: Marla Gibbs. You may recognize her from the tv shows 227 and the Jefferson's. She was my patient over 15 years ago and we have remained friends ever since. She just received the Hollywood Star of Fame in July 2021. I flew out there with my boyfriend, Dr. Jeffry Lapsker, to support her. Helping a patient regain strength, function, and nutritional needs are priceless for better quality of life. She taught me to be grateful and Thankful. Grateful that I chose to spend many years studying so I was able to help people get healthier naturally and Thankful that she was a patient that wanted to work beside me on her health journey. She turned 30 for the 3rd time. Her wisdom has taught me that it is never too late to start or even restart your health journey.

I find that more women take the initiative to get healthy, compared to their male counterparts. It is nice to see when the men are ready to make a change. I had a male patient who was a CFO for a large company. He informed me that he was doing everything his doctor told him to do and his medications were getting increased with no further health benefits. He was a diabetic with neuropathy in his feet, had high blood pressure, high cholesterol, and decreased sexual desire. He was married for over 28 years and of all the things he wanted help was his desire to make his wife happy. The first thing I had to do was educate him about the main difference between a functional medicine doctor and a conventional medical doctor. We both use the same numbers when looking at blood labs; however, a functional medicine doctor will look at smaller ranges, so we are able to do prevention with the patients as opposed to re-action. After a few months of treatment, his neuropathy was gone, he no longer needed his statin or high blood pressure medicine, and his blood sugar numbers went back to clinically being a non-diabetic. All these things were helpful in him regaining his desire again with his wife. I got a "Thank You" from her!

When I say "Thank You" to people, it can apply both personally and professionally, it is not always a "positive" statement.

Let me explain. I was married and when that didn't work out, my reaction was all 5 of the stages of grief:

Denial: I was in shock, I had rushes of overwhelming emotion. That was my defense mechanism. When I was home, I was able to let it out and think. When I was at work – I had to keep it professional, moving forward.

Anger: Because I was not prepared for that decision. After all, I am a well-educated female. How did I miss the "signs?" ...

Bargaining: I was going to make different decisions in the future. Because now I am smarter and I'm in control of who I allow to take my power away. I needed to get the negative self-talk out of the way.

Depression: That feeling of "Am I good enough for anybody at this stage in life? I have helped so many patients and friends and why couldn't I help myself? I felt regretful and I didn't like that about myself. I had many times of writing letters and releasing all the negative words on paper into the fire pit. I felt cleansed.

Acceptance: This one is the best of them all. I had to accept the reality of my loss. It couldn't be changed. I could still feel sad, and I was moving forward. There could still be triggers that popped up on an Anniversary date or even a Facebook memory. The days when I could read about them and smile instead of cry told me how far along I had come from flip-flopping through the stages.

Each time I had a personal loss and experienced grief, I had to go through these different stages. Some took longer than others to be able to move on. That is where "Thank You" is necessary to believe in your gut that whatever happened, I learned the life lesson to say those beautiful words. I got through it. Sometimes it took months, others it took years. It is not a race to see how fast one can get through all these stages. Some days I was experiencing a couple at the same time. Everyone grieves differently. For me, it is being able to say "Thank You!" for the good and the bad that happen. I can be a better friend, mentor, and doctor. I can empathize as well as sympathize with people.

When you are dealing with life's struggles, take a step back and analyze what happened and how you can learn from it. Be Thankful for the lesson. When you are dealing with another person, you don't have to go into detail as to "why" you are thankful for that experience. Just say "Thank You" out loud and the words and sentences that you are thinking after that can be silent. And then you smile, because you are the only one who knows the rest of the sentence.

When everything is in a positive trend, don't forget to say "Thank You."

DR. KIM MARTIN, DC

D r. Kim Martin, DC has over 24 years of experience improving the lives of her patients, using an all-natural holistic approach. She takes time to analyze your symptoms and develops an overall wellness plan, getting to the root cause of your health concerns. Telemedicine is available.

Connect with Dr. Martin here https://NorthShoreHealthSolutions.com.

CHAPTER NINETEEN

RELEASE TRAPPED EMOTION: YOUR KEY TO WELLNESS, SUCCESS, AND HAPPINESS

by Laura Sharp-Waites

Life & Business Accelerator & Founder, Heart Unburdened

https://heartunburdened.com

We all start somewhere. I don't know how this book got into your hands. I don't know where you are on your wellness journey. Maybe you're struggling through a season of dreams that didn't come true? Are you dealing with the loss of health? Maybe you are weary, wounded, and angry that God hasn't seemed to follow through for you. Whoever you are, and wherever you're coming from, I'm so glad you're here. It's time to release those trapped emotions that may be setting you up for failure.

My life was going along as most people's – work, family, pets, friends, church, hobbies, and if time permitted, self-care. We understand the value and benefits of self-care, but rarely plan for it and do it. Once a year, we women should go and have a physical and the dreaded mammogram. Who wants to go and have their boob squished and smushed? Certainly not me! Looking back, I am so glad I did endure the squish and smush as it saved my life!

On July 31st, 2017, my life was forever changed. That was the day I received my breast cancer diagnosis. My husband, Todd, and I were still in the newlywed stage as we had not even been married for 2 years. Cancer was nowhere in either of our vocabulary. Yet here I was with Invasive Ductal Carcinoma (IDC) breast cancer. It was an aggressively growing form of cancer and needed to be removed ASAP!

Probably like most people, I never fully knew what was involved in having cancer. I had known people who had been diagnosed, but I never knew what having cancer would mean to me and my family. About 1 in 8 U.S. women (about 13%) will develop invasive breast cancer over the course of her lifetime. In 2021, an estimated 281,550 new cases of invasive breast cancer are expected to be diagnosed in women in the U.S., along with 49,290 new cases of non-invasive (in situ) breast cancer.[1]

In case no one has told you, cancer is not just a diagnosis, it is a journey! It's not like getting Strep Throat with everyone receiving the same prescription. Instead, each person's journey will be different as we are each uniquely made. By this I mean there are 8+ types of breast cancer in women including Invasive, Invasive Lobular, Triple Negative, Inflammatory, Angiosarcoma, Ductal Carcinoma in Situ, Lobular Carcinoma in situ, Paget's Disease, and a number of rare types.[2] Add to this Estrogen Receptor-positive (ER+) and negative (ER-), Progesterone Receptor-negative (PR-), and HER2 receptor-negative (HER2-) and it gets more confusing.[3] Since we each have our own DNA, no two people's cancer will be the same and neither will their treatment.

This chapter is designed to highlight wellness. You might think all I need to do to avoid getting cancer is eat right, exercise, stay away from harmful chemicals, and have good genetics. However, many more factors affect whether or not you will get an illness such as cancer. Surprisingly, this includes grief.

Are you grieving something that happened in your life, something really important to you? Every loss we experience is grief, and we've all experienced a number of losses over the past few years with the COVID-19 Pandemic. These losses are varied and could include a change of job, moving or a change in housing, divorce, or a death of a loved one.

For me, my grief was the death of my first husband. It was a bit stressful, to say the least. Immediately after his death, a number of issues and challenges came to light. He had been hiding financial dealings, covering up and doing things in secret that weren't right. This included not paying bills or not sending checks after I had written them. It was a big mess.

Within 24 hours of his death, I went from grieving to pissed off to beyond angry. I did go through a grieving process, and even though I had done quite a bit of grief work, what I had done didn't prepare me for this situation.

My body had no clue what to do with my emotions, anger, and frustration. I ended up stuffing those emotions down in my body because I didn't think I could share them with him, obviously, because he was now dead. How do I deal with all of this?

According to WebMD, when grief is not properly dealt with, it can cause sleep problems, fatigue, lowered immunity, inflammation, anxiety, high levels of cortisol over a long period can raise your chances of heart disease or high blood pressure, digestive issues, various body aches and pains, higher risk of heart attack, unhealthy coping mechanisms, and mental health challenges.[4] Also at this time, I had trapped those emotions, in the form of anger and frustration, deep in my body, where they started to cause health issues.

Some emotions I was dealing with were jealousy (of other people's lives), longing (for my life to get back to normal), overwhelm (from all of the secrets, packing, moving, and with paperwork after someone dies), shame, pride, and humiliation (upon learning bills I thought were paid had not been), and feeling unworthy or worthless (second-guessing my choice of husband).

It's not surprising my body reacted. According to Dr. Bradley Nelson, these specific emotions are thought to become trapped in the glands or sexual organs.[5] In my case, the right breast.

While I did have some genetic links to the mutation that caused breast cancer, I honestly feel that 99% of my cancer was related to trapped emotions because I did not deal with my grief adequately. Not only did I not deal with it at the time, I also didn't fully deal with it when I thought I was addressing it.

What does that mean? Well, I actually went and participated in an evidenced based grief program, Grief Recovery Method®, which helped me immensely. I worked through so many issues, thoughts, and memories. I was able to think of him with fond memories instead of wanting to kill him. It helped me so much that I went on to become certified as a Grief Recovery Method Specialist.

Despite all of the grief work I did, I never really got down to working on the trapped emotions. I did forgive him. Forgiveness is for us, the living. In this case, my person was already gone. Forgiveness is much healthier for us.

To deal with the remaining trapped emotions, I chose the method of the Emotion Code™. I ended up working with trapped emotions, specifically some of those emotions that I mentioned earlier. Imagine that I had really low vibrating emotions including shame, which is the lowest vibration there is. Imagine that these negative emotions are in your body. They were good sized, dark, hard, and icky. As previously mentioned, the trapped emotions I had were trapped in my right breast where they stayed, growing, and becoming an aggressively growing cancer tumor.

In my journey, I have done the basic and advanced grief work, along with Emotion Code™ sessions. I worked on a wall of emotions called a Heart Wall that surrounded my heart protecting me from being hurt again. This Heart Wall was focused on my late husband and as I started releasing the emotions making up this Heart Wall, I started seeing my health improve. As I continue my Emotion Code™ sessions, I have included healthier food options, more movement, additional rest and sleep, and tons of self-care.

Todd and I recently celebrated our 5th wedding anniversary and I am proud to say I am almost 3 years cancer free! It was a journey we didn't ask for, yet it taught me so much. I use all that I have learned to help my clients achieve success, become happier and healthier, and experience freedom from those trapped emotions that threaten their wellness.

Help yourself by taking a few minutes and an inventory of what's going on within yourself. Do you have any trapped emotions? Are you aware of any trapped emotions?

People lack an understanding and awareness of trapped emotions. A trapped emotion can be something a teacher spoke about when you were in grade school such as you'll never amount to anything, you're not going to make the team, you're not good enough or pretty enough. The list goes on; not skinny enough, not fast enough, etc. Sometimes it's a parent who told you that you'd never amount to anything because you didn't get good grades. Maybe it was a well-meaning friend who said are you actually going to wear that out in public? Or gosh, that outfit makes your butt, hips, boobs, or whatever look bigger, worse, or ugly. You become self-conscious. They planted that seed.

Maybe it's a spouse who has said things to you. If you were starting a business they could have said something like what makes you think you can sell something or you can run a business? So many seeds are planted that sprout and root and grow into trapped emotions.

These comments sound harmless. Your family and friends likely mean well. They love you, but don't realize what they're saying is terribly harmful to you. These icky emotions start from that small seed.

Most are unaware these comments are impacting your life, your business, and your family. Trapped emotions affect your mindset. They affect how you see yourself, how you handle money, how you raise your children, how you are in a relationship, and how you move forward in life. These all impact your mindset. If any of those aspects are out of alignment, they can and will cause issues and often physical ones.

Don't take the long route like I did. Press forward and get some help.

If you're thinking, WOW is this for real? Yes, it is. If you don't know if you have any trapped emotions, I encourage you to take this free quiz to see if you have trapped emotions that could be holding your life or business back. Find the free quiz at http://heartunburdened.com/tw-quiz. You will receive immediate results and have the opportunity to sign-up for Free Emotion Code™ Tools that will be delivered to your inbox. These tools can help you start to identify and remove your trapped emotions. This is a tool I wish I had had for myself.

How else can you help yourself achieve better wellness?

In moving forward, learn to deal with your emotions immediately when something happens. If you're having a bad day, take a moment wherever you are to take a deep breath and think about it. Is it really important to trap it in your body or can you just let it go? You can make that choice.

Part of working with the trapped emotions and moving forward is acknowledging them. Honor that they exist. Honor them because they have allowed you to learn lessons. Then release them. These trapped emotions no longer serve you. In fact, in some cases they never served you and it's time for them to go.

You can live a healthy life. You can eat healthy. You can take all the right supplements. You can exercise. You can do the right thing. For the sake of your own wellness, take it a step further and get rid of your trapped emotions. They could be harming you. You deserve to live your life to the fullest. The best way you can do that is to re-lease trapped emotions, and create your own wellness, success, and happiness!

[1] https://www.breastcancer.org/symptoms/understand_bc/
statistics

[2] https://www.cancerresearchuk.org/about-cancer/breast-cancer/
stages-types-grades/types

[3] https://www.komen.org/breast-cancer/diagnosis/
factors-that-affect-prognosis/tumor-types/

[4] https://www.webmd.com/mental-health/ss/
slideshow-grief-health-effects

[5] Nelson, Bradley. *The Emotion Code: How to Release Your Trapped Emotions for Abundant Health, Love and Happiness.* Random House, 2019, 193.

LAURA SHARP-WAITES

Laura Sharp-Waites, M. Ed., MDiv., Ed. D Life & Business Accelerator, Founder of Heart Unburdened, and Host of Embracing God's Purpose for Women.

Helping people has always been a gift for Laura. For many years, she was a Special Education Teacher and a College Professor, supporting people of all ages and walks of life through a myriad of personal, professional, and spiritual struggles.

Laura's life changed dramatically when she faced a battle with breast cancer. During the diagnosis, a pre-cancerous tumor was found on an ovary. While having something removed that could cause additional cancer seems like a great thing, it also meant the end to the dream of Laura and her new husband Todd having a biological baby. As a result, Laura experienced major grief over the loss of her ovaries. Laura's healing was the catalyst that propelled her into further training with the Grief Recovery Method® where she became an Advanced Grief Specialist and Discover Healing where she became a Certified Emotion Code Practitioner in The Emotion Code™.

Laura now blends her extensive educational experience and certifications to help her clients. Laura holds a number of certifications, a Master's in Special Education, a Master's in Divinity: Pastoral Counseling, and a Doctorate in Organizational Leadership.

Connect with Laura in the Embracing God's Purpose for Women Community https://bit.ly/EmbracingGodsPurpose at
https://heartunburdened.com.

CHAPTER TWENTY

LIVING FULLY - FROM THE INSIDE-OUT

by Lesley Klein
Co-Founder, Legrity Media LLC
www.legritymedia.com

During college in the late-'80s, I was introduced to a completely different set of health and holistic practices. This introduction led to my own personal philosophy called Inside-Out. In my studies, I learned about the scientific reasons as to why meditation works to reduce stress, which is one of the bottom-line causes of many dis-eases. I also learned about the concept of Wellness as opposed to health. The concept of Wellness sees human health not only in terms of physical health, but includes several other areas of Wellness: Spiritual, Emotional, Intellectual, Social, Environmental, Occupational, and Financial.

Here are the definitions of each sector in the eight-part Wellness Wheel*:

- Physical Wellness - recognizing the need for physical activity, sleep, drinking water, and nutrition.
- Spiritual Wellness - the ability to establish harmony and peace in life and have meaning and purpose.
- Emotional Wellness - the ability to cope effectively with life and create satisfying relationships.
- Intellectual Wellness - recognizing creative abilities and expanding knowledge and skills.

- Social Wellness - the ability to relate to and connect with others in society.
- Environmental Wellness - creating pleasant, stimulating environments that support well-being both personally and globally.
- Occupational Wellness - the ability to get personal fulfillment from jobs or chosen career fields that are in line with one's mission and purpose.
- Financial Wellness - the ability to identify your relationship with money and develop skills in managing resources.

* Wellness Wheel from www.scafp.org by Dr. Peggy Swarbrick, creator of *8 Dimensions of Wellness: Physical, Emotional, Spiritual, Financial, Environmental, Occupational, Social, and Intellectual*

Viewing our being in this holistic way made total sense to me and this model of Wellness has stayed with me ever since. I also learned later that our body is not just made up of the Physical body, but we also have an Emotional body, a Spiritual body, and a Mental body that makes up who we really are as an energetic being. I agree with the belief that we are eternal spiritual beings having a temporary human experience and not the other way around.

So, seeing my wellness as a balance of these eight areas has helped me to live life more holistically and happily. I strive to live a life of balance and from the inside-out… What do I mean by inside-out? Well, since Thoughts lead to Emotions which leads to Action and then Results, I believe our well-being starts from the inside and is reflected in our outer world. Being aware of our Thoughts is the starting point and realizing that we are in control of our Thoughts is empowering. Taking responsibility for our Thoughts and ultimately our precious life on this planet and this existence is where the breakthrough can happen from Victim to Victor. This means taking responsibility for the good, bad, and ugly we have created in life. Yes, even the things that we can't imagine we would have attracted to ourselves! I do believe in the Universal Law of Attraction that says "like attracts like." Knowing and working with this principle is the key to creating the life we want to live. Heaven on Earth is possible, one person at a time.

When the "Great Pause" of 2020 happened, I was introduced to the Healy, a German-made device that uses frequencies to balance and harmonize the physical, mental, emotional, and physical bodies! It became available that year in the United States. In December of 2020, I was also offered the opportunity to produce and host my own digital TV show, called Good-Vibes.TV which focuses on ways to "raise your vibe and thrive." Then in 2021, I co-Founded a digital TV network called Legrity.TV (mashup of Legacy & Integrity) with four other co-Founders. Besides producing my show, I am now able to empower others with their own TV show on our network that "positively impacts lives and communities."

In my show, Good-Vibes.TV, I teach people about their energy field… helping people, like yourself, understand that our bioenergetic field reaches 8 feet out from our center and consists of our physical, mental, emotional, and spiritual bodies. On Good-Vibes.TV, I interview different experts about ways they raise their vibration to create the world they want. Basically, the Law of Attraction principle in action. The Law of Attraction is the universal principle that says "like things" attract "like things." So focusing your mental energy on love will bring love to you. However, focusing on a Lack of love will only bring you less love in your life. Don't believe me? Try it for yourself! Use a Gratitude Journal for 30 days and see if that doesn't completely change your life.

Let's go down the Quantum Physics rabbit hole: everything has a vibration… everything vibrates at a frequency. Dr. David R. Hawkins describes the range of the vibrations of emotions from shame (20) and guilt (30) … to love (500), gratitude (510), and peace (600) with Enlightenment ranging from 700 to 1000 on his Map of Consciousness scale (0 - 1000).** He states how the majority of society operates below 200 on this scale, ping-ponging between humiliation (20), fear (100), hate (150), and pride (175). The Law of Attraction says that *like* attracts *like*, so to attract abundance, you need to be *feeling* abundant… in a state or frequency of abundance, not lack or scarcity.

MAP OF CONSCIOUSNESS

	God-view	Life-view	Level	Scale	Emotion	Process	
	Self	Is	Enlightenment	700-1000	Ineffable	Pure Consciousness	
	All-Being	Perfect	Peace	600	Bliss	Illumination	
	One	Complete	Joy	540	Serenity	Transfiguration	
P O W E R	Loving	Benign	Love	500	Reverence	Revelation	S T R O N G
	Wise	Meaningful	Reason	400	Understanding	Abstraction	
	Merciful	Harmonious	Acceptance	350	Forgiveness	Transcendence	
	Inspiring	Hopeful	Willingness	310	Optimism	Intention	
	Enabling	Satisfactory	Neutrality	250	Trust	Release	
	Permitting	Feasible	Courage	200	Affirmation	Empowerment	
	Indifferent	Demanding	Pride	175	Scorn	Inflation	
	Vengeful	Antagonistic	Anger	150	Hate	Aggression	
F O R C E	Denying	Disappointing	Desire	125	Craving	Enslavement	W E A K
	Punitive	Frightening	Fear	100	Anxiety	Withdrawal	
	Disdainful	Tragic	Grief	75	Regret	Despondency	
	Condemning	Hopeless	Apathy	50	Despair	Abdication	
	Vindictive	Evil	Guilt	30	Blame	Destruction	
	Despising	Miserable	Shame	20	Humiliation	Elimination	

**Map of Consciousness Chart by Dr. David R. Hawkins from <u>Power v. Force</u>

Have you ever had a bad day that kept getting worse the more you reacted negatively to the string of unfortunate events? That's the Law of Attraction in action but NOT working FOR you. To stop the negative chain of thoughts in your head, you must first be aware of what you are thinking! Be aware. Then breathe… After a couple of deep breaths (I recommend 10 in and out), you shut down the flight/fight reflex that was triggered by the first unwanted occurrence. Once out of the panic mode, you can be aware of your reaction, or reactionary thought, and stop the domino effect. Laugh at the occurrence. Affirm the opposite of the occurrence. Shift your state, your vibration, and you gain control again. You are the Captain of your ship, so take the helm.

Abraham, through Ester Hicks, talks about the 22-step scale of emotions on her Emotional Guidance Scale. The chart has fear/grief/depression/despair/powerlessness on the bottom at #22 with boredom (8) then contentment (7) in the middle and joy/appreciation/empowerment/freedom/love at the top of the scale (1). She states you can only incrementally move up the ladder, so find where you are on the scale and focus on the next feeling up the scale till you are ping-ponging in the "Feel Good" range. Focus on raising your emotional vibration and stay in the "Feeling Good" emotional range between 1 and 7; not in the "Feeling Bad" emotional range between 8 and 22.***

From the book "Ask and It is Given" by Abraham-Hicks - www.abraham-hicks.com

	EMOTIONAL GUIDANCE SCALE		
Manifestation Zone	1	Joy/Appreciation/Empowered/Freedom/Love	FEELING GOOD
	2	Passion	*Your desire is about to manifest*
	3	Enthusiasm/Eagerness/Happiness	
	4	Positive Expectation/Belief	
	5	Optimism	*Vibrational Matches start showing up here*
	6	Hopefulness	
	7	Contentment	
	8	Boredom	
	9	Pessimism	
	10	Frustration/Irritation/Impatience	*Resistance to your desire manifesting has 'cleared up' at this point*
	11	Overwhelment	
	12	Disappointment	
	13	Doubt	FEELING BAD
	14	Worry	
	15	Blame	
	16	Discouragement	
	17	Anger	
	18	Revenge	
	19	Hatred/Rage	
	20	Jealousy	
	21	Insecurity/Guilt/Unworthiness	
	22	Fear/Grief/Depression/Despair/Powerlessness	

inwardquest.com/questions/5901

***Emotional Guidance Scale by Abraham Hicks from <u>Ask and It is Given</u>

So, once you notice where you are vibrating: "Oh, I feel fearful when I see a low bank balance or when I get an unexpected bill." Breathe and affirm: "All is well in my peaceful and prosperous world!" Say it out loud, with feeling and even movement, if possible. Keep saying it, until you FEEL it. Visualize what that would mean in your life right now. Taste it. Smell it. Hear it. Feel it. Then bask in the feeling of a higher vibration. Move on with your day. Listen to the internal promptings of things you can do to improve your financial situation. You have just changed the trajectory of your day! Make this a habit and you are golden! You never have to be a victim of negative circumstances again. You can master your life when you master your thoughts.

Going back to the Wellness Model... I practice meditation and journaling for my spiritual and emotional wellness... yoga, bicycling, and walking for my physical wellness. My TV show and network plus investment into cryptocurrencies assist in my Financial Wellness. I love to read and learn which serves in my Intellectual Wellness while my work with Good-Vibes.TV and Legrity.TV aid in my Social, Occupational, and Environmental Wellness. I love working in my Peace Garden (shaped as a Peace sign) growing herbs, vegetables, and flowers which assists with my Physical Wellness and Environmental Wellness. This is how my individual wellness has evolved to date.

What about you? Take a look at your life through the eyes of this Wellness Wheel and assess how "well" you are.

Are some areas full but others less attended to?

This model is just a guide and there are no hard and fast rules. It is totally up to you to create a life of Wellness and happiness.

One thing I learned along the way was not to worry about the problems of the world but to focus on creating the best life possible for me because I can only be responsible for myself. As each of us takes individual responsibility for ourselves and grow and thrive, we energetically help improve the whole. Connect with your Higher Power and follow your intuition... take Divinely inspired action and love yourself! Also, love others and help them by your example. Don't get caught up in the drama on TV, the internet or other people's lives that lowers your vibration. Step back and focus on what you can change and improve in your life. You deserve to live a life of Wellness... to thrive and be the best possible version of YOU from the Inside-Out!

LESLEY KLEIN

L esley Klein is the Producer & Host of a Digital Television talk show called *Good-Vibes.TV* (2021) which focuses on ways to "raise your vibe and thrive." She has a Masters Degree in Mass Communication from Towson State University and a BS in Broadcast Production from the University of Florida.

Ms. Klein is also a contributing author in two International Best-Selling books: *1 Habit for Entrepreneurial Success* (published 2020) and *1 Habit for Thriving in a Post-Covid World* (published 2021).

She has been an entrepreneur for over 27 years. She created and operated an award-winning metaphysical bookstore in Florida where she was immersed in the world of crystal vibrations and energy for 16 years. Her own personal spiritual journey led her to become a Reiki Master, an aromatherapist, and a meditator. Using these natural means, she learned how to raise her vibration and maintain wellness as well as create a life of her dreams!

Her mission is to raise the vibration of the planet, one person at a time. What she loves most about what she does is seeing her human and animal families thrive because of the information and the Healy that she shares.

When she is not producing her talk show, she is hiking the forest on the mountain where she lives or biking with her husband of 27 years… or earthing herself in her Peace Garden with her two rescued fur babies, Penny and Murph!

The best way to reach her is at https://LesleyKlein.com.

CHAPTER TWENTY-ONE

OVERCOMING THE DARKNESS WITHIN

by Michael Stanley
Coach, Mentor, Speaker, Author

A chieving and maintaining wellness has become a huge part of my journey throughout life. It's allowed me to attract health, happiness, and so much more into my existence. But wellness is so much more than good health; it's a state of being, it's becoming aligned and connected to your true self, mind, body, and soul. It's becoming who you were meant to be, fulfilling your purpose here on earth, and allowing yourself to become one with the energy that connects all living things. Wellness is about overcoming the obstacles that hold you back in life, it's about doing what's right, what's true, and what will make you feel most alive. Achieving wellness is a life-changing experience, it'll allow you to transform the perception of yourself, of the world, and of others. In order to change our lives, we must learn to change ourselves.

Achieving wellness in my life has been years in the making and has taken so much time, effort, and patience to get to where I am today. It hasn't been an easy road, and I've spent most of my life walking through darkness, through heartache, and through pain. But life isn't always about the destination, it's about the journey. One of the most important lessons I've had the opportunity to learn is that everything that we experience along the way is what makes us who we are. A life without trials and tribulations just doesn't exist. We are constantly blessed with opportunities to learn, grow, and evolve. Sometimes it just takes a change in perspective and some hindsight to help us understand that most of the things we go through are pivotal life lessons. Change your perspective; change your life. It took me a long time to grasp that concept, but it's helped pave the way for so much opportunity and personal growth. Our viewpoint on the things we experience and go through can heavily determine the outcome and the way our lives turn out. Life is precious, it's a gift, a blessing, and none of us really know how much life we have left to live. So live with everything you are, and everything you have, strive for greatness, and strive for wellness because these are the most important gifts you can bless yourself with.

For as long as I can remember, I've struggled with depression and have been broken and consumed by darkness. It took me a long time to find the light, to regain my energy and my power. As I look back, I can see that I had no concept of self-love. I was doing everything that I could to numb the pain that I felt inside, to hide the depths of my sorrows. I was burying it all deep within myself as an attempt to run from my problems, but this just made my depression even worse. I felt a void within myself that I couldn't seem to fill, no matter how hard I tried. I was struggling to find my way in the world, to figure out who I really was, and if my life had any meaning. Little did I know, my search for something deeper would eventually end up being the key to setting myself free.

One thing I've learned is that life tends to align us with the path we're meant to walk whether we're ready or not, and if we stay stagnant for too long life might find a way of pushing us in the right direction. Life provides us with the opportunities we need to evolve, and sometimes if you don't act on life, life acts on you. That's exactly what happened to me—life decided to push me out of my comfort zone, and with that push came something significant and life changing, but probably not in the way you expect. At the age of twenty-four, I suffered a serious spinal injury and was diagnosed with an L5S1 disc protrusion. This experience changed my life and my perspective on everything. It was the beginning of my breaking point, my rock bottom. So on top of my depression, I was now dealing with the most intense physical pain that I've ever felt in my life. When I say it was life changing, that's no exaggeration. I couldn't sit, I couldn't lay down, I was more than uncomfortable, and for the following few years, that was my life. In pain, every second of every day with no relief, no matter what I tried. I was told by several doctors that without a major surgery I could potentially have permanent nerve damage and lose feeling from the waist down, and even with surgery there was a chance that the pain wouldn't subside, and that I would be forced to live with limited mobility. I did not like those odds, but those are the cards I was dealt. On top of it all, and shortly after my injury occurred, I lost my job and my health insurance, so surgery or even seeing a doctor was out of the question.

These were the darkest moments of my life and at that time I had never felt more hopeless. The black cloud surrounding my being just seemed to keep getting darker. It felt as if my spirit had been shattered into a thousand pieces. I was completely exhausted, inside and out. But it was in these moments, at the peak of my dark night of the soul, that something inside of me began to shift. I'm not sure if I was just in denial about the situation, but I refused to accept the fact that that was to be my fate. Something inside of me just knew that I had the ability to heal and to overcome what I was experiencing. This is when I learned the importance of believing in oneself and the true power and capabilities of the mind.

It felt as if my soul had risen from the ashes and said enough is enough, and it was in these moments that I knew that I needed to make a decision. I could either give up, or do everything in my power to change my circumstances because I knew I couldn't go on living the way I was for much longer. I made the decision that giving up was not an option. Thankfully, I decided that my life was worth fighting for. I made a promise to myself that I would do whatever it took to overcome what I was going through, and to become the person I knew I was capable of being. From that moment on, my life has never been the same.

This is when I learned that sometimes the greatest blessings in life can be disguised as the worst of circumstances, that all it takes is a shift in perspective and your entire life from there on out can change. To change my life, I had to change myself, I had to change the way I was living, the way I was thinking, I had to change my perspective and my beliefs about myself and of the world. I began to have faith in the journey and I realized that the only way out was through. I started to confront my demons, my fears, and everything I had buried within myself for so long. I came to understand one of life's hardest truths, that nothing or no one was going to save me, that I had to learn to save myself.

I began to put wellness at the forefront of my life. I spent day in and day out working on myself as I rehabilitated my body and developed my character. I had to learn to rewire my mind, to operate differently. I knew that in order to change, I had to change, and that wasn't easy by any means. I began by addressing all of the bad habits I had acquired and everything I knew was holding me back in life, then integrated healthy habits and behaviors in their place. I had to learn to improve the way I spoke about myself, to myself, because the thoughts and emotions we have about ourselves and our lives can heavily determine our outcome. I changed my diet and started noticing significant results in the state of my mental and physical health. I started exercising my body and developed a plan and the discipline to stick to it. I began to meditate on a regular basis, to help focus and develop my mind. I read and listened to motivational content every day as a way to educate myself and acquire as much knowledge on self-improvement as I possibly could. I began to develop my spiritual nature, my philosophy, and my outlook on life. Which put me on the path to finding my truth, my meaning, and my purpose. Developing my philosophy helped me realize that by asking questions and searching for knowledge in regard to reality and human existence, we open ourselves up to our understanding of this world and our place in it. Everything I've been through has helped me understand that how we comprehend our reality and ourselves will help determine how we process our experiences, and ultimately how we live our lives. I dedicated all of my free time to improving myself in any way that I knew how. I changed myself inside and out. It was a process that took so much time, effort, patience, and dedication, but I started to heal and as I began to notice an improvement it became addictive, it became a way of life. The key to the prison I had created for myself all those years ago was me all along. Once I stepped out of the darkness and into the light, I knew there was no going back.

A big part of achieving wellness is having the ability to understand that everything that we experience is an essential part of our journey. The things we go through are meant to help guide us towards our physical and spiritual evolution. My injury taught me the importance of health and physical well-being, that if you believe in yourself, anything is possible and achievable. My depression taught me the importance of perspective and the power of the mind. That the good and bad times are what makes us who we are, and what makes us human. The struggles we face help us appreciate the good times, and the hard times help us to learn, grow, and to evolve. As hard as it was, I wouldn't trade those experiences for the world. They've made me stronger, wiser, and ultimately into who I am today.

No matter what has happened or where life has led you, don't ever give up hope, don't ever stop fighting for what you believe in, don't ever stop searching for the light no matter how dark your world may seem. It's not what happens to us, but how we choose to react that defines who we are. As hard as it may seem, speak the life you wish to live into existence, learn how to be the hero of your own story. Learn to follow your heart, to walk with faith, and to find a way to electrify your spirit and bring energy and love into your existence. Do what makes you feel most alive, because that's where happiness is found. Life is short, it's precious, and it's a gift, so don't ever take it for granted. Wellness isn't something that just happens overnight or instantaneously, it's something that one must pursue and consistently work towards. Wellness is something that must be maintained, it's a lifestyle, a choice, an attitude, and a way of being. So fight for what you know you deserve, accept the challenges life puts in your path, and if darkness finds a way into your existence, do whatever it takes to find the light.

MICHAEL STANLEY

Michael Stanley is a speaker, mentor, author, coach, and wilderness survival instructor. His mission is to teach self-empowerment and self-development techniques to anyone struggling to improve their lives and find their way in the world. Michael shows people how to connect to their roots, to nature, and to overcome the darkness within themselves. He's passionate about helping others grow through what they go through and to find meaning, purpose, and direction in their lives. He currently resides in Houston, Texas, USA where he spends his time exploring the mysteries of the universe and encouraging others to find their path and to become who they were meant to be.

You can connect with Michael here:https://facebook.com/mstanley25.

CHAPTER TWENTY-TWO

FROM SHATTERED TO WHOLE

by Paige Davidson
Founder, Fasting with Paige
www.FastingWithPaige.com

A life of struggling with obesity, then morbid obesity, left me feeling shattered as a woman. No area of my life was left unscathed. From my confidence to my self-esteem, from my ability to feel like a competent professional despite my education and advanced degree, to poor health in every category, the struggle to feel normal felt never-ending.

I felt the effects of this struggle daily. I was despondent that I couldn't control my weight. I felt physically and emotionally drained, my joints ached, I developed obstructive sleep apnea. I was embarrassed about how I looked and I had no confidence in myself, despite many other accomplishments in my life. My social life, spiritual health, emotional and mental health, and of course my physical health were all negatively impacted by my excessive weight.

As a child I was a normal weight, but a family history of morbid obesity left my mother struggling to find a way to prevent me from following her own difficult path. Out of love and concern for me, she often admonished me about the food I was eating or wanted to eat. What was genuinely meant to help me, instead set up a lifetime of struggle with food. Starting in high school, if not middle school, I began the roller coaster of dieting, weight loss, then regain. Yo-yo dieting became my normal from an early age.

For most of my adult life, I bounced from one weight loss program to the next, always searching for what was finally going to work, feeling more desperate with every attempt. I tried every physician's weight loss center, weekly weigh-in program, gym, doctor prescribed weight loss medications, liquid diets, diets that cut out entire food groups, and every fad diet that came along. With each effort, I lost weight and followed that diet until I couldn't stand it anymore. The weighing and measuring, the food logs, the counting calories or macros and micros, the lists of good and bad foods, the extreme actions required by the diet. Then I would quit, return to the way I was eating before, and gain the weight back plus more. With each failed attempt to lose weight for good, my self-esteem fell a bit more, until it eventually bottomed out. I literally **DIETED MY WAY UP TO 315 POUNDS.** Yes, you read that right. Dieted my way UP in weight. I hit rock bottom emotionally and, out of desperation, in 2000 I agreed to undergo gastric bypass surgery.

I was given a tool to help me lose weight, but was not given what I really needed, help in finding out why I struggled so much with food and weight gain. I followed the guidelines from the surgeon to the letter and over 18 months lost 150 pounds. I was elated, but a nervous wreck at the same time. Following the surgery guidelines over time was like hanging on by my fingernails. I maintained that weight loss for about five years, but eventually I started the dreaded but anticipated slow weight regain. I had never been able to keep weight off before, and I didn't see how this was going to be any different.

By 2019 my weight was back up to 249, and I was once again having health problems. I had to have a knee replacement and my other joints were aching as well. I had to wear a CPAP machine to sleep due to obstructive sleep apnea. Worst of all, I had developed two highly painful foot conditions, plantar fasciitis and Achilles Tendonitis. My job required me to be on my feet at all times, and I was literally limping in pain. I was dangerously close to becoming unable to do my job, which was terrifying.

Taking Drastic Action

Until this point, I had been chasing "skinny." Society said you were of value if you were thin, so that was always my goal in trying to lose weight. But something inside of me changed. Whereas for years my focus was on trying to look better, my goal became to actually feel better, and get healthy, in all areas of my life. I wanted to be in balance physically, emotionally, mentally, and spiritually. I wanted holistic health and wellness.

My first action was to declare that I was never dieting again. Dieting had caused me to weigh over 300 pounds, then lose a great deal of weight only to gain it back. I knew the food wasn't the problem. Of course I didn't know what the problem was, so I decided to do the one thing that I had never tried. To find out what the root of the problem was, to discover why I had spent my life struggling with food instead of utilizing it to nourish my body.

I decided to seek counseling to find out what was really happening with me. I found an amazing Christian counselor. Spiritual health was at the top of my list and where I chose to begin my healing process.

While we were doing the work of discovering why I had such issues with food and weight, I was introduced to an eating practice called intermittent fasting. It was new to me, and when I heard that it involved eating only for a certain amount of time each day and the rest of the time was spent fasting, eating no food at all, I declared I would never do that! It sounded like a crazy fad diet, and I was never dieting again. When I learned that it actually wasn't a diet at all, and that it heals inflammation in the body, I decided to research it further. Both of my painful foot conditions were caused by inflammation. Through research, I discovered all of the health benefits of intermittent fasting, and because I was so desperate to get out of pain, I decided to try it, with my counselor's blessing.

Intermittent Fasting Spurs Holistic Wellness

I began my intermittent fasting practice in June of 2019. There was no way that I could physically exercise… I could barely walk. But I could determine which hours during the day that I would eat my food, called an eating window. And I could practice a clean fast outside of my eating window. During a clean fast, there are five acceptable beverages that don't break your fast: black coffee, plain water, unflavored sparkling water, plain black tea, and plain green tea. I hit the ground running and began with a daily 19-hour fast and a 5-hour eating window. It was so hard at first, and most people start much more slowly. But my most immediate goal was to get out of pain, and a 19- or 20-hour fast, for most people, is an excellent protocol for both internal healing and weight loss. After a week, I went to a 20-hour daily fast.

And it worked! Within two weeks, I wasn't limping anymore. I was elated! I was still experiencing pain, but it was reduced enough that I could walk normally. I kept going, and after three months of intermittent fasting my research had revealed that when focusing on healing the body, longer fasts are appropriate. So, I began doing one 42-hour fast per week, and my regular 20-hour fast the rest of the week. Again, the first few weeks it was very difficult, but I was determined to heal my inflammation. By the time I had been practicing intermittent fasting for 6 months, my foot pain was 100% cured. I was not only no longer in pain, but I had also lost almost 60 pounds. By not dieting, but naturally making healthier food choices and following an intermittent fasting protocol every day.

Eventually, within 14 months of beginning intermittent fasting, I had lost 110 pounds. At this point, I was down 176 from my highest weight of 315 pounds.

As I continued to work on my spiritual health through prayer and developing a closer relationship with Jesus, intermittent fasting and exercise had given me excellent physical health. After losing 60 pounds, I added walking and light weight training to my routine, 5 or 6 days a week. Starting with just 20 minutes a day, I eventually worked up to walking 3 to 6 miles most days. My obstructive sleep apnea was healed and I no longer required the use of a CPAP machine to sleep. My joints no longer ached. I could walk up several flights of stairs without getting winded. People kept telling me how beautiful my skin looked. I had energy to burn and my sleep was much improved.

Through the practice of intermittent fasting, losing 110 pounds, and counseling, the other areas of health were also healed.

Emotionally, I learned to truly love myself. I learned to treat myself like my own best friend, and become my own best advocate. I began to really focus on self-care, and as I did my self-esteem and confidence grew exponentially. I became empowered to make good health decisions for myself, and I learned to trust myself. Over the years I had become convinced that there was nothing I could do to help myself and I had been overcome with a victim mentality. Now, through experience, I realized that I absolutely could make good decisions for myself. I no longer wanted to spend most of my time alone. I discovered that once my confidence and self-esteem were restored, that I truly enjoyed spending time with friends and family.

All of these gains greatly boosted my mental health. For years I suffered with depression and took medication for it. As I healed both physically and emotionally, I found that I no longer needed one medicine for depression, and my doctor reduced a second medication. I reveled in the fact that I had become resilient and strong, determined to make the best choices for myself. Experience taught me the importance of daily healthy habits, and how vital they are in living a healthy lifestyle. Choosing healthy and delicious foods to keep in the house and eliminating lots of processed foods and sweets was an excellent habit that I developed, and helped to contribute to my success. With every positive step I took, my mental health grew stronger.

What had started out as a desperate attempt to reduce foot pain became the key to discovering holistic health. Intermittent fasting was not only the vehicle to heal my body physically, but was the impetus to do the work to find ways to take care of myself emotionally, spiritually, and mentally. These days, I feel whole. All areas of my life are in balance, and I feel happy, deeply happy, for the first time in my life. When I began this journey, I had no idea the healing that would take place for me, but I am deeply grateful; to God, to the discovery of the amazingly healthy practice of intermittent fasting, to my skilled and empathic Christian counselor, and to the strong woman that I have become. She has been here all the time, through thick and thin, and is truly my strongest ally.

Today, my goal in life is to give back. To help other women who have faced a lifetime of struggle with obesity and morbid obesity. Women who have been through the devastating experience of losing weight with gastric bypass surgery only to gain it back again. To show women that menopause can truly be the best time of your life, that you are not doomed to having a spare tire and exhaustion forever. No matter your past experience, you can find health and happiness in all areas of your life, and I am there to coach and guide as many women to finding that success as I can. I became a certified health and life coach, specializing in intermittent fasting and mindset work, in order to help me reach that goal of helping others find the contentment and peace in their life that I have found in mine. You CAN do it!

PAIGE DAVIDSON

Paige Davidson is a survivor of morbid obesity, a multitude of failed diets, and even failed gastric bypass surgery. After 40+ years of suffering, she finally became empowered to take her health into her own hands. Ditching diets forever and living an intermittent fasting lifestyle, Paige has lost a total of 176 pounds and healed several obesity related health conditions. She is a certified health coach, has written several books, and started a virtual coaching business. Paige has been featured on the cover of Woman's World magazine and has also been featured in a special edition of Woman's World: Women over 50, Half their Size!

You can connect with Paige here https://fastingwithpaige.com.

CHAPTER TWENTY-THREE

YOU ARE UNIQUELY DESIGNED AND BUILT FOR A PURPOSE

by Prophetess Nalo Thomas Mitchell
Founder/President of Nuggets With Prophetess
Nalo Ministries

I was blessed to grow up on the Southside of Chicago and later the Northside of the city as an only child in a loving family. My maternal Grandmother (Grammie) lived just a few blocks from my Mother and I, and she was very instrumental in raising me. Although I grew up in a single parent home, I was fortunate to have a close relationship with my Father (who later remarried my late Step-Mother) because he made me feel as if I was the apple of his eye along with my sister and brother.

My Mother made sure my life was well-rounded. She was a full-time physical education and dance teacher. As a passionate dancer, she was a member of the Joseph Holmes Dance Theatre and they performed in quite a few prestigious venues in Chicago, including: The Auditorium Theatre, Kennedy King College, Navy Pier, and National Louis University. Growing up around the Arts, along with my paternal grandmother and aunts who took the time to nurture me, helped to shape and mold me into the woman I am today.

As a child, I'd hear my elders refer to life as a marathon and not a sprint. It wasn't until many years later that I would come to understand the meaning of that statement. Life is a marathon and a journey. Each day has its own worries, but if we want to win in life we must cast our cares on our heavenly Father because he is concerned about the things that concern us.

The vicissitudes of life consist of ups and downs, but we must continue to strive for excellence and choose joy. Joy is one of the keys on this journey called life. If you look at the cup as half empty, then life will be half empty. However, when you choose to look at the cup as half full, then life will be full because you made a conscientious choice of joy.

Joy will change the trajectory of your life and you will begin to soar and win in areas where you previously lacked strength. Continue to press, push, and pray as you look to succeed and win in life. You will overcome all obstacles that come your way and you shall win.

One day while purchasing beauty products, an elderly woman shared the analogy of life with me in this way, "In your 20s life goes twenty miles per hour, in your 30s life goes thirty miles per hour, in your 40s life goes forty miles per hour" (so on and so forth; you get the drift). As the years began to pass, I would understand this analogy in a deeper depth. Children get older (as do we), grandchildren are born, parents and loved ones pass away, and our bodies begin to change. As I age, my ultimate goal is to care for others with more compassion and win others to Christ and be well.

I encourage you to prosper in all things and be in good health even as your soul prospers. That's one of the key elements to winning in life, being in good health. When we are well and whole, we attract others who desire to be well and those who are well; then we all win!

It had been two decades since I had been what one would consider an athlete. Track and field was the sport in which I participated during my elementary school years and throughout my entire high school career. As an adult, the only running I did was running from the house to the car. In 2002 I expressed to my family that I intended on running in the Chicago Marathon.

I was completely stoked to share the news with everyone. I'll never forget that sunny afternoon as we stood in my Grammie's kitchen in the family building that she purchased in the late 1980s. We lived in a 3-flat brownstone in Rogers Park and as we stood in my grandmother's kitchen, she exclaimed, "You can't run a marathon, you might die." The fact of the matter was that there were runners who had passed out and the news had reported athletes who had passed away after running a full marathon. So, I decided not to pursue this goal because I didn't want my Grandmother to worry about her only grandchild passing away. So, I put my desire on the backburner because I wanted my entire family to win and if that meant making sure others were at ease with certain decisions I made, then I was willing to make the sacrifice.

Winning is often the ultimate goal in today's society. We are told to be the best we can be and encouraged to be number one and told that number two isn't winning. However, this mantra isn't true. Winning is a mindset! Winning involves finishing the race in which you are called to! Of course, there are some sports where finishing in second place means you haven't won, but our goal should be finishing strong, giving 100%, and working in a spirit of excellence.

Winning involves finishing the race in which you are called to. Strength resonates differently from one person to the next. Let's take for example running a half marathon. I had the pleasure—or rather I was insane and decided to train and run a half marathon in 2011. As a former high school track and field athlete who despised long distance running, I made up my mind to run the race and, with the support of my family, I trained for a total of four months.

The day came and it was time for me to run 13.1 miles in the Lincoln Half Marathon. I had trained with one of my friends from church and on the day of the race, our pace wasn't grooving (maybe it was my adrenaline, but it just wasn't lining up). I prayed and needed guidance on how I could finish the race and finish strong.

I was perplexed and bewildered by the number of participants and felt led to run with a couple who seemed to have a rhythm that I could glean from and I decided to follow their lead. They explained their strategy and I was all in! Their strategy was to run one mile and walk 30 seconds. This was a game changer for me. I had never used this plan of action while training for the race, but it worked. I had my playlist in my ears, energy chewables in my pocket, and water on my hips. All of these things determined my roadmap to success. I encourage you to be flexible and strategize your roadmap for success and winning.

You see, I wasn't trying to outrun anyone or finish first in any category. Winning for me simply meant sprinting the last block in an effort to shave a few seconds off my time while finishing strong and crossing the finish line.

Strong for me was different from other runners. Some people had previously run this particular race and desired to slash their time by seconds or minutes and then there were those, like me, who defined finishing strong and winning as completing the race.

Winning takes time, grit, prayer, determination, and a mindset that says, "I'm not giving up no matter what." We can talk and think about our goals all day long, but we must remember, "Faith without work is dead." We must write the vision and make it plain. We must have our roadmap and plan of action. Action and faith go hand in hand when it comes to winning.

There were times when I felt like throwing in the towel as I trained for the race. I was working full time, married, and had three children who were still school age, as well as serving in ministry. But, I was challenged to work through the obstacles. I was encouraged not to give up. I'm thankful for the encouragement and that I stuck with my goal, determined strategies of success, and was a winner because I finished the race!

As a person of faith, I believe that it's pivotal to:

- Determine the heavenly strategies we need in order to win in life
- Pray until something happens, even when we're uncomfortable and faced with obstacles
- Press into the goal, lean and walk in our Kingdom Purpose
- Push until the right door opens on our behalf

Oftentimes society confuses being the best by comparing themselves with others, be it a neighbor, friend, family member, or someone they see on social media. When I was growing up, we didn't have a microwave oven and popcorn was made on the stovetop and it took time because you had to make it in the skillet or a popcorn popper. You needed oil (Crisco was popular back then), popcorn kernels, a skillet, and the skillet top to seal the kernels as they popped.

You had to execute a precision of shifting the skillet as the popcorn kernels turned into popcorn. Then once this process was completed, the popcorn was placed in a bowl and you were able to add salt, pepper and butter and whatever seasoning you desired in order to make your popcorn just right for you and your family. Sometimes, the popcorn wouldn't turn out just right if you left it in the skillet too long. Or you would have to wait a little longer if you didn't allow the oil to get hot enough before adding the kernels.

But, back then we didn't give up because we wanted our snack. It may have taken 10 to 15 minutes to make it on the stove (along with gathering all the supplies), but you made the best of it. The popcorn wasn't like it is today, where you place a bag in the microwave oven and within a matter of minutes it's ready with the seasoning, butter or flavoring already sealed in the bag. Preparing popcorn in the skillet as opposed to in the microwave takes more precision and time (much like our goals).

Goals don't have the microwave effect. People don't just wake up and say I'm going to run a half marathon and do so the next day without proper training. Much like preparing for a half marathon, it takes strategizing, training, proper hydration, healthy eating, and wearing the appropriate attire.

You may be in a dry season in your life, or you feel like giving up on some of your goals because the preparation and opposition are greater than what you anticipated. Remember, don't give up and don't give in because in the end you will win! Keep your mind on things above, keep your kingdom purpose close to your heart, and watch the shifting that begins to resonate in your life.

Awesome, Beautiful, Beloved and Loved; that's who you are! Do any of these terms of endearment sound familiar to you? I certainly hope they do because you are a masterpiece created by God to conquer giants, defeat obstacles, live above only and not beneath and soar. Remember, you cannot be duplicated or replicated because you are uniquely designed and built for a purpose in which only you can fulfill! Even if you don't feel like a winner, remember … you are winning! Continue to walk by faith and not by sight. You are triumphant and remember when you pray, press, and push, you will conquer the obstacles in life! You are a winner, be well!

WIFE * MOTHER * PROPHETESS * SPEAKER * GOD'S GIRL

PROPHETESS NALO THOMAS MITCHELL

Prophetess Nalo Thomas Mitchell is the wife of Elder Darrell Mitchell. She is a Mother, Yaya, ordained Prophetess and an Anointed Woman of God who believes in empowering and encouraging others to reach their Kingdom God-given purpose. She is a born again believer who gave her life to Christ in January 1996. She believes that when you are steadfast before The Lord, you'll learn that you are an amazing masterpiece, born in the right place at the right time for God's purpose! She has never met a stranger and loves to uplift others.

Earning a Bachelor of Arts in Broadcasting from the Walter Cronkite School of Journalism at Arizona State University in 2007, she went on to further her education and obtained a Masters Degree in Organizational Leadership and Change from Colorado Technical University in 2013. Prophetess Nalo was honored to become an ordained Prophetess of the gospel in 2017 under the leadership of Table of Life

Ministries and an ordained Pastor in 2021 at Faith Community Center in Springfield, Illinois.

Prophetess Nalo is the Founder and President of NWPNM, Nuggets With Prophetess Nalo Ministries in Springfield, Illinois, where her family roots date back to the 1800s. NWPNM launched in 2020 as a not-for-profit organization created for charitable and educational purposes to empower others while sharing the gospel.

You can connect with Prophetess Nalo here: https://facebook.com/ProphetessNalo.

CHAPTER TWENTY-FOUR

HAPPY BEING WELL

by Rita Farruggia
Founder & CEO, Happybeingwell.com
www.Happybeingwell.com

When you think about the way you live, do you feel content? Do you feel fulfilled? Do you feel happy about where you are now? Or, perhaps you feel like you are not feeling your best and as though you could be happier. We have all been there – including myself. We all have times throughout our life that make us feel like there is something missing. This feeling is one we can change by taking the right steps! When you put yourself first and be happy, the world gives back to you because you are able to give happiness to others. Doing wellness practices in your day-to-day life, you are much more likely to get successful results in all areas of your life because when you are happy, you are more productive, attractive and can think better versus being unhappy. An unhappy person's brain is tired, has poor memory, poor concentration, poor focus, lacks creativity and is unmotivated.

I am a passionate advocate for happiness because there was a time in my life where I didn't have the clarity to see the little goals that needed to be achieved in order to achieve my big goals, staying in toxic relationships, and letting the thoughts of fear hijack my internal compass. When a compass isn't working, it is not letting you know where you are in order to get to where you want to go. When I wasn't thinking clearly,

I thought having something external outside of me was the answer to massive success and happiness. It wasn't until I looked within myself to give myself the gift of happiness, trust, and peace that came from clarity. It was a journey to reach the realization that we are the only ones who know what is best for us and to cultivate the practice of listening to our intuition and trusting it. It is only then that we have the strength and faith to take the right actions with persistence regardless of what we hear around us, it is then that we become unstoppable to win. Due to the happiness, peace, and clarity it has brought me, I decided to develop a company that is devoted to being happy being well. So, I named my company, HappyBeingWell.com.

I want to spread the awareness to love yourself by giving yourself the gift of happiness through doing wellness activities daily, which brings clarity. I have curated the best quality organic products to support wellness activities.

This chapter is all about bringing happiness into your life by incorporating positive habits of wellness. The result? Happiness within your life to be a winner. The strategies discussed below will increase your happiness. How do I know? I incorporate it into my daily life and I am happy being well.

Meditate: Rewire Your Brain for Happiness

Meditation is a powerful way to improve your focus, energy, sleep, mood, creativity, clarity, and concentration. Meditation has also been proven to increase our happiness. In a study published in *Psychiatry Research: Neuroimaging*, it was stated that after participants meditated regularly, parts of the participants' brains associated with compassion and self-awareness grew, and parts associated with stress reduced. When I started meditating many years ago, it was a challenge to meditate due to an active mind. I have learned to use aromatherapy, essential oils, crystals, candles, hot luxurious baths, meditation music, and guided meditations to go into a deeper meditation much more easily. Depending on what type of meditation I am doing, I use different types of essential oils, crystals, and candles. If I am doing a self-love meditation or compassion for others meditation, I use a rose quartz crystal that I hold in one hand and in the other hand a clear quartz crystal. Rose quartz is known as the love crystal as it is known to release a love frequency and I chose clear quartz in the other hand because it increases the frequency of the crystals around it and increases mental clarity. I love burning sage as I meditate as the smell of sage calms the nervous system down and increases concentration. Plus, looking at the swirls of smoke swirling in the air puts you into a trance. I also rub lavender essential oil mixed with a carrier oil like coconut oil to apply on my forehead and temples to further help calm my mind to easily get into a meditative state. If I am not burning sage, then some days I put lavender oil in my aromatherapy diffuser to enhance my meditation. There are so many wonderful essential oils to try in your aromatherapy diffuser to experience the scents you love the most or stimulates the most happiness. Peppermint oil is known as the happy oil as its smell uplifts your mood. I recommend using a diffuser. For more information about the benefits of each essential oils and different ways to use them in your daily wellness practises, you can download a free copy of "Essential Oils Guide" at happybeingwell.com/collections/resources on the resources page under Blog. I also use candles when meditating because I love staring into the candle flame, while watching the flame dance around. It puts me into a meditative state before closing my eyes, plus the wonderful smells of a vanilla, apple cinnamon, jasmine, or lavender candle is calming. There is something magical about lit candles. You can also set an intention during your meditation. For example, if you are seeking the right decision about an important matter, set the intention for clarity. If you are looking for a guided meditation on achieving higher levels of success, you can listen to the episodes titled,

"Achieve Higher Levels of Success With This Meditation Now" and "Abundance/Wealth Meditation" on the, "Happy Being Well" podcast on Apple iTunes and/or Spotify.

I love making a luxurious hot bath filled with organic bath goodies. Taking a long hot bath is an easy hack to meditate because the warm water immediately calms down your nervous system. I add bath salts, organic bath bombs, natural bath oils, and a crystal to increase muscle relaxation. My favorite crystal to add to my bath water is a tumbled rose quartz, or tumbled amethyst crystal. I light candles around the bathtub and on my bathroom vanity counter. I also light sage incense. I turn on meditation music and turn the lights off leaving only the candle light to light up the bathroom. This creates a tranquil environment. Plus, you get the added perk of adding moisture to your skin to get a youthful glow after your meditative bath session when adding bath bombs and bath oils to your bath water. If you want to learn more about meditation techniques, you can download a free copy of "Meditation Made Easy" e-book at happybeingwell.com/collections/resources. Plus, you can get 15% off all natural products mentioned above using code: winner15 with free shipping in the USA at Happybeingwell.com.

Use Affirmations to Rewire Your Brain for Happiness

I use affirmations to overcome limiting beliefs with empowering beliefs to propel me into action mode because when we believe in ourselves, we make things happen. It also feels good when you feel good about yourself because you allow yourself to be happy with yourself. This is where magic happens because we take massive action on our creative ideas when we believe in ourselves. Chanting affirmations has increased the quality of my life because they have empowered me to take massive action that leads to achieving more progress in all areas of my life and that leads to winning in life. Using affirmations daily gave me the courage to create my company, Happybeingwell.com and to stay persistent in growing the company.

We all have days when we may feel overwhelmed or low. Simply by saying out loud in repetition, "I am healthy, I am happy, I am smart, I am confident, I am fearless, I can do it" makes me feel a shift in my body and gives me more energy. I say my affirmations as part of my morning routine when I apply my all-natural facial mask because the natural mask feels soothing on my skin so it puts me into a relaxed state. Saying affirmations in a relaxed state makes affirmations more powerful because you are better able to counteract the chatter of your mind, and the suggestion behind the affirmation will move from the realm of thought into the realm of feeling more quickly. When I use an all-natural facial mask, it has healing soothing properties when applied to the skin. You feel more relaxed due to the soothing sensation of the natural ingredients plus the soothing sensation of massaging my face with the creamy texture. You can find an all-natural facial mask in our beauty section on Happybeingwell.com.

How Affirmations Rewire Our Brain

You may not believe it at first, but the constant repetition causes the affirmation to be meaningless and its implication doesn't jar. It starts to feel natural to say it, and you feel comfortable with it. Since the statement is familiar, the left side of the brain no longer needs to analyze it and it passes to the right side of the brain. The right side is not concerned with judgment, only emotion and sensation. It will accept the thought without question and transform it into a positive feeling. Fears of not being enough or failure will dissipate, and a new self-confidence will emerge. When I first learned how to first identify my limiting beliefs, I was able to craft affirmations specific to overcome my limiting beliefs of not being good enough. One way I discovered my limiting beliefs that dwelled in my subconscious that was affecting my actions or inactions in life was to ask myself why I was making certain decisions then writing down the answers. Once you discover your specific limiting beliefs, you can flip it around. For example, if you believe you are not strong enough, say in repetition, "I am strong enough". For more techniques on how to overcome limiting beliefs, you can download a free e-book on "How to Overcome Limiting Beliefs" at happybeingwell.com/collections/resources.

Physical Exercise Makes Us Happy

Exercise improves our well-being, including reversing the effects of aging, since physical exercise improves brain performance. It also makes us happy because when we exercise it releases serotonin (happy brain chemical). In my early adulthood, I would resort to comfort food as the quick and easy fix to soothe stress, which lead to weight gain. This changed when I learned how to cook plant-based meals and woke up at 5 am in the morning to jump on my stepper for 20 minutes followed by 15 minutes of meditation every morning to feel good at the start of my day. Plus, do yoga after work to release stress of the day. Eating plant-based food helps me stay consistent with physical exercise since it gives me more energy and I lost the extra weight, which also increased my energy levels. If you are looking for plant-based recipe ideas, you can download a free Plant Based Recipes e-book at happybeingwell.com/collections/resources.

I love doing wellness activities because it activates higher levels of growth and progression in all areas of my life. The common denominator to success, love, joy, and peace is the quality of our relationships: the relationship with ourself, our significant other, friends, employees, colleagues, clients/customers, children, etc. When we feel good with ourselves and we are fully aware of ourselves, we are better communicators and can connect deeply with ourselves and others allowing for better cooperation on all your life projects. For more free wellness e-books, you can visit our collection at happybeingwell.com/collections/resources. I highly recommend downloading a free self-care journal from Happy Being Well that has 51 powerful questions that helps to get to know yourself better, your desires, gifts, and manifest your desires into reality. You can download it in our resources section as well. Enjoy your wellness journey.

RITA FARRUGGIA

Rita Farruggia is a self-care/ self-love/happiness expert. Rita is the founder & CEO of happybeingwell.com, which is a wellness e-commerce site devoted to providing organic self-care products to amplify your wellness so you can be happy being well. HappyBeingWell.com has a mission of being the #1 Self-Care Community in North America.

Rita's mission is to awaken people to their love, teaching them how to reprogram their subconscious to align with truth through creating a daily self-care practice. It is through a commitment to a daily self-care practice that we can eliminate the noise of the world, stress, anxiety, and our rapid thoughts. This allows us to be able to align with our personal truth, love, clarity, focus, intuition, and confidence. This process allows us to know who we are, deepens our compassion and ability to love ourselves and others. This is the reason Rita is committed to providing the best natural products you will love to use and wear whether it's luxurious active-wear leggings to work out or meditate in, clean skincare, or creating a luxurious at home spa feeling with salt lamps, crystal book-ends, aromatherapy diffusers, natural essential oils, natural candles, all natural facial masks, crystals and much more at Happybeingwell.com. HappyBeingWell.com offers the tools/products, free educational resources, and inspiration to use in your daily spiritual and wellness practices.

You can connect with Rita here https://Happybeingwell.com.

CHAPTER TWENTY-FIVE

WELLNESS HEALS

by Romy Faith Ganser
Practitioner, Romy Faith Wellness
https://Linktr.ee/RomyFaith

A series of events at the turn of the century hit my life like an earthquake; they knocked down the walls and shook my footing. My brother passed after battling Leukemia and a year later my husband and I divorced. I went from being a happy, active stay-at-home mom of a 5-year-old boy to being a frazzled-single-Mom-working-a-full-time-job-40-minutes-away. My daily angst was being late to aftercare pick up...again.

Soon after, I was invited to attend a Christian Renewal weekend. This overworked, really frazzled, holding on by my nails, single mom was dead-set against it. I arrived home from those three days with a whole new faith. I knew that God was with me to heal my broken heart and my crushed spirit.

"For I know the plans I have for you," declares the Lord, "plans to prosper you and not to harm you, plans to give you hope and a future." Jeremiah 29:11

On a beautiful morning in June 2002, I arrived to work with a few minutes to spare. I decided on a large, iced coffee and muffin from the Dunkin' Donuts. As I was exiting, a man held open the first of two doors. I smiled, thanked him, and proceeded to catch my foot under the mud mat.

The hand holding the coffee made a grab for the handle on the second door. I broke my shoulder on the doorframe as my head hit the door.

I was in shock, sprawled half-in and half-out with my sundress around my waist, lying on my muffin, and covered in my favorite lite-n-sweet. Folks climbed over and around me until someone directed the uncaffeinated masses to the drive-thru.

I was laid off six months later, January 2003. Soon after, I had an MRI to help diagnose numbness in my hand. In addition to physical damage, the test revealed that I had Multiple Sclerosis. I sold my house in Rhode Island and moved home to Connecticut. There, I consulted with many specialists, one who diagnosed Chronic Lyme Disease. It was indicated that the CLD caused the MS. This is a controversial theory even today. Consultation with a Naturopath revealed I had developed the Chronic Lyme Disease from a hornet sting when I was ten. Six months of daily IV antibiotics treated the CLD so that I could then start my MS protocol.

The year 2003 was tough for me and my family, but I approached my future with a positive attitude. I was determined to get back to work. My background was in event planning and sales and marketing. I walked with an unsteady gait that was a turnoff at interviews. I had trouble accepting my new reality. Having worked in the hospitality industry for thirty years, I had taken some hard falls on wet floors. The days of bouncing up and back to business were over. The falls continued. Now I was really hurting. Doctors gave me a pat on the shoulder and told me," You'll be wheelchair bound in two years" and "You have MS Dear, you're going to have to get used to the pain." I refused. This pain was not going to stop me. I was even so determined to be able to get onto the lacrosse field to watch my boy play that I bought myself a wheeled walker for my 38th birthday.

I was determined to resume normal activities, so I headed to a springtime craft fair. As I was pushing the walker through the grass,

I came upon Dr. Mathew Paterna of Shoreline Family Chiropractic. He was very friendly, so I stopped to chat. I explained my condition and that I had seen many Chiropractors. My back hurt more after the adjustments than before. He said he might be able to help me. I'd heard all that before. I thanked him and continued on my way.

The summer was coming to an end. I was serving on the board of a non-profit that was holding a Health and Wellness fundraiser. I entered the exhibit area pushing that wheeled walker and immediately met eyes with Dr. Matt. "Oh no, maybe he doesn't recognize me," I thought. I knew full-well he did.

In October, my mother called and asked me to attend a talk being given at the Vitamin Shoppe regarding Fibromyalgia. Guess who was giving the talk? This third time around Dr. Matt and I shared a good laugh. I gave God a little thank you realizing this was His plan. Dr. Matt asked if he could demonstrate on me. He then massaged my neck below my ears explaining that he was massaging the ducts that carry fluid along the spinal column, keeping it lubricated. He shared that when your body experiences trauma like my falls, the ducts sometimes get kinked like a garden hose. The gentle massage helps to loosen them and then lubricates the spine. And maybe relieves some discomfort. Wow! Already I was feeling some relief from the chronic pain!

Dr. Matt had been treating me three times a week for several weeks when he asked how I was feeling. I told him I was feeling better and was overjoyed about the impact his massage was having on my pain level. "I am so passionate about the work you're doing," I said, "I want to work here." He chuckled, taken aback by my reply. My pain level continued to drop and I got increasingly better over the next few months. One day, Dr. Matt asked, "What else can I do for you, Romy?" "I want to work for you," I stated matter-of-factly. He took a moment and went on to say that it's not good practice to hire patients. I understood. Until a few weeks later when I overheard the Marketing Coordinator saying that she would be leaving. She arranged for Shoreline Family Chiropractic to participate in community events. This was my opportunity. I came into my next appointment with my three-page resume in hand and again announced that I **really** wanted to work there.

The call came the next day. I had gotten Dr. Matt's attention! "You are definitely qualified for the job, Romy, but I'll be honest with you," he said, "There's a lot of equipment and supplies we need to move." We have to make sure you can handle the job physically. We met at a two-day event so I could observe what he does. I arrived the second day with some of my own equipment. I brought with me a folding wagon for moving supplies. I brought a folding bar chair to eliminate having to lift from a standard chair. I also brought bed lifts to lift the table to counter height. This equipment made it more comfortable for me to share with potential patients about the body's innate ability to heal itself when given the proper environment. I was explaining that by getting regular spinal adjustments, you are empowering your central nervous system to keep the body functioning at its most optimal ability. Chiropractic adjustments can help to relieve many conditions without the use of medications. Some are sinus headaches, infertility, depression, and ADD/ADHD and many more.

At the first major community event, the team and I signed up forty new patients. I was delighted. I was using my story to save people's lives. I continued to have great success in building relationships and using my story to educate people. I even arranged for Dr. Matt to give free weekly Lunch-n-Learn presentations at Whole Foods. A great opportunity for patients, but now I was moving and setting up movie screens for PowerPoint presentations. Unfortunately, my success impacted my physical condition, requiring me to move on after a year of working with Dr. Matt. I have learned so much from him, my mentor and my friend. Thank you, Matt!

Now the challenge was to figure out what to do with this new knowledge I had.? I found the Institute for Integrative Nutrition. The year-long online program was exactly what I had been looking for. Not only was I going to be able to improve my own well-being, but help others do the same. I earned my Certification in Holistic Health Coaching.

In 2007, I had had surgery on my neck as a result of the-fall-that-started-it-all. At that same time, my neurosurgeon, Dr. Kenneth Lipow of Bridgeport Hospital, said the condition of my lumbar spine wasn't "bad enough" to warrant surgery. "Call me when the nerve pain is shooting down both legs," he instructed. Now it was 2012, the pain I felt in my right leg was worse when I was walking. My biggest relief came through my MS yoga classes. I wanted to focus my practice on Holistic Pain Management in an effort to help myself and others manage their chronic pain. With that in mind, in 2017 I registered to Certify in Yoga Therapy. I had to drop those plans when, two classes into the training, I woke to find I couldn't feel from the waist down. The neurosurgeon said it was my hip. The hip doctor said it was the back and the MS doctor said, "Romy, you do too much." Three weeks in rehab and twelve weeks of physical therapy left me no closer to relief. I was mad now. I wanted answers.

Trust in the Lord with all your heart, and lean not on your own understanding; In all your ways acknowledge Him, And He will make your paths straight. Proverbs 3:5-6

In complete frustration, I called a pain management doctor. This doctor looked at my old MRIs for three minutes and said, "You have a cyst pressing on your spine causing stenosis." With tears of relief in my eyes, I went home and called the surgeon. The back pain had finally gotten BAD enough. Besides the cyst and stenosis, they found a herniated disc and a degenerative disc. It had taken ten years.

The surgery fused three low lumbar discs. I felt great. I certified to teach Chair Yoga. I was sure I had finally found my purpose, my WHY.

The problem was I still kept falling. I was on a medication that helped people with MS to walk faster, but when your body is compromised but your head wants to walk faster you fall instead. I stopped taking those meds, but the damage was done. I now had another herniated disc, my pelvis twisted, and I was literally crooked. The surgeon urged me to seek physical therapy before rushing into another surgery. I was lucky to have consulted with the MS Foundation and found MS specialist Leigh Ronald, Ph.D. of Sacred Heart University and Carolton Outpatient Therapy. She and her team have been instrumental in strengthening my body and getting me moving again! Thank you, Leigh!

After a year, I again sought the surgeon's evaluation. I had to show him that my pain was not a result of scoliosis, but was a surgical issue that he could fix. I wore that hard bubble-gum-pink scoliosis belt for six months. It was my only relief. Finally, in 2021, I had yet another spinal surgery. My back is now fused from my waist to my tailbone. I'm straighter than I've been in twenty years, but, more importantly, I'm pain free. The nerve connections are cleared and I walked so well right after surgery that I didn't need rehab. My heartfelt gratitude to Dr. Lipow.

As this chapter closes, I see a bright new one beginning. My hope is that you have seen a little of yourself in my story and have been inspired to persevere where you may have grown weary. If any of my experience resonates with you or a loved one, I invite you to contact me. I am happy to elaborate on any of the topics I've shared.

Wellness happens when the mind, body, and spirit are balanced. Then the healing can truly begin. Wellness Heals…

ROMY FAITH GANSER

Romy Faith Ganser, BS, Holistic Health Practitioner, is a graduate of the Institute for Integrative Nutrition where she earned her certification as a Holistic Health Coach. Romy also holds certifications in Chair Yoga Instruction and Reiki I & II. With these credentials, Romy has gained experience in patient advocacy, one-on-one and group counseling, and health education presentations. Her passion has long been to share her knowledge of the body's innate and robust ability to heal itself. By aiding clients to better understand their physical, mental, and spiritual needs, she works with them to find their individual, optimal health. After graduating from Johnson and Wales University with a BS in Hospitality Management, she went on to spend three decades in the service industry, starting in food and hotel services, and then moving on to conference, event, and trade show planning. Her skills of interpersonal communication, attention to detail and marketing, along with her thorough understanding of healthy food preparation and overall health education background, form a perfect foundation for Romy's position as a Holistic Health

Practitioner. Romy holds memberships in several professional organizations, including her local Chamber of Commerce, Foundation for Wellness Professionals, and the American Association of Drugless Practitioners.

You can connect with Romy here: https://Linktr.ee/RomyFaith.

CHAPTER TWENTY-SIX

THE REMEDY TO LOSING MONEY AND RECLAIMING YOUR POWER

by Sabrina Protic
Financial Coach, World Class Partners Associates
https://www.sabrinaprotic.com/

Financial Wellness is Power. When you lose control of that power, you may experience an unhealthy state of mental and physical weakness. The symptoms may include headaches, loss of appetite, overeating, body aches, brain fog, nervousness, anxiety, edginess and isolation. In some cases, loss of financial power has taken a toll on relationships, family, friends, and business associates. Have you ever felt the strain of not being in control financially?

As a Financial and Life Coach, I empower people to take their power back. What do I mean by that? There are scenarios in our lives that sneak up on us. Have you ever felt rejected because you did not get the raise you were expecting, or the job offer that you felt most qualified for? Or perhaps you unexpectedly lost a career job after many years of service leaving you financially deficient. We oftentimes succumb to our emotions of disappointment, emptiness, anger, and frustration. The secret to overcoming these negative feelings is retaining your power with proactive thinking.

How many times have you heard it said that we should all have a Plan A and Plan B? I am here to tell you that you also need a Plan C.

Plan A is income, whether for employment or entrepreneurship. Plan B is the safety net when Plan A is depleted or removed entirely. Both Plans A and B are "now money" needed for survival. Plan C is what you and your family will need to survive in the distant future, perhaps retirement or a health issue limiting your ability to physically work to earn income. Let's call this your Financial First Aid Wellness Kit. What's in your kit? Do you have Plans A, B, and C?

My first big financial injury happened before I knew it. I suffered a huge blow when my career job of 41 years came to a sudden end due to pandemic cutbacks. My first reaction was "Wow, is this really happening to me?" I had been a stellar employee and had my vision set on working another three to five years. It was surreal. My husband and I were not financially prepared for this. Has anything like this happened to you or someone you know? It leaves an empty feeling in your gut. Yes, remember the symptoms of losing your financial power and money. I did have a Plan B, but the pandemic cut that off, too. About six months prior, I had become a Certified Life Coach, which involved face-to-face contact and public speaking. Of course, all of that was squashed due to sheltering in place. Plan A gone and Plan B crushed. I had not seen the wisdom of establishing a Plan C. At my age, Plan C would have been healing and the antidote. Technically, I should have been able to transition right into retirement, but I was not prepared.

What would you have done in this situation? Here's what I did. I shifted into power mode. I did not focus on my job loss or my employer. I did not agonize over not being able to move forward in public spaces with life coaching and public speaking. I began to design my financial future to protect my well-being and at the same time help others. My inner voice said "no more employment." My new purpose will be coaching the community on building a sound financial safety net." One of the secrets to overcoming life challenges is helping other people. I also had to set an example for my adult children that were watching me walk through this fire. They needed know that fire will come their way, too, but to be prepared with a fire hose.

Some of the most impactful leaders are those who have gone through the fire and survived to tell their story to empower others to avoid similar paths. I had put all my eggs in one basket and thought that I would depart my company on my terms. I thought that within the following three years that I would have ramped up my income to life changing status as I entered the world of public speaking, book writing, and book tours. Of course, this experience gave me something to write and speak about. I pictured myself sitting on the beach in the Caribbean sipping my favorite concoction post-employment. That was a dream without a plan. Have you been negatively affected during challenging times? Did it affect your health, mind, and body? After bombing, like me, some people are now booming because they retained their power with great resiliency.

Take time to evaluate the "what-ifs." Are you prepared? What if you lost your job and you are close to retirement, could you retire? What if the major breadwinner fell away in death or became critically, chronically, or terminally ill and could not work, would your household survive financially? Or simply, what if you want to stop working altogether, have you set up multiple streams of income? How can Plan C help? It's setting various money strategies for financial security at any age or stage in life. This could include residual income, investments, retirement income, life sustaining savings, certain types of insurances, and eliminating debt. We also refer to this as a financial game plan. This is where the power comes in as a proactive approach to establish another layer of income sourcing. I encourage you to take control of your family, your life, and your future.

What is your relationship with money? I encourage you to have a healthy view of money and its role in your life. When I was a kid, we were taught to save our allowance in a piggy bank. In a sense, this was the beginning of a financial game plan. I was thrilled to purchase an organ for $60 with money I had saved. As a young adult, I paid cash for my first car, a 2-door sporty Mercury Comet. Remember, part of Plan C is eliminating debt. My parents did a good job of teaching us to live within our means. However, when I married and started a family, we fell into the credit card trap. I say trap because banks were giving credit cards out like candy. No one taught me how to manage credit and debt. Our household was financially sick for years in the vicious cycle of charging, making revolving payment, and never seeing the balance go to zero. When I lost my employment income, we still had debt. This was not a good situation. The only saving grace was the severance pay that I received after my termination. We bailed out of all debt except our mortgage, a silver lining. Money definitely played a role in our sheer survival and recovery. We still needed to bring in life sustaining income for daily living, but we were one step closer to financial well-being.

Reverse your thinking that an employer, family member, or wishing for windfall of cash from the lottery is going to supply income when life events occur. This is giving away your power and is financially unhealthy. Financial Wellness is a daily awareness of your assets, liabilities, and keeping track of the money trail. I recall someone sharing a story that a family member had passed away and the insurance company informed the family that the policy had been depleted resulting in zero death benefits. How did this happen? No one was doing a yearly policy review. This policy review should include updating assigned beneficiaries. Why are we talking about life insurance? When a household income earner passes away, the income is lost. Oftentimes, the surviving spouse or partner struggles financially and this is complicated when there are minor children involved. Have you ever seen this happen? Do you see the physical and mental toll this takes on the surviving spouse or partner? Or has this happened to you? Plan C could be the remedy in these circumstances.

Do you have an executable Will in place? Have you found yourself trying to backtrack and fix something like this? Setting up a will means that you retain the power over your assets and that your wishes will be carried out for your estate. Have you thought about who will be responsible for your debt or home should something happen to you? Who will care for your spouse or minor children should the unthinkable happen? There are plenty of cases where a Will cannot be located or if one ever existed. Sometimes a questionable Will magically appears, perhaps it's handwritten, very old, not dated, and the signatures are not verifiable. These situations can wreak havoc on families. Consider reviewing your Will and naming a trusted person as the executor of your Will. Secure your Will, life insurance policies, and other important legal documents in a safe place such as a bank safety deposit box. Ensure that someone else other than you has access to the safety deposit box and, as always, consult with an attorney for the laws in your state.

Your Financial Wellness is directly tied to relationship changes. When I went through a divorce, I was so overwrought that I neglected to update the beneficiary information on my 401(k) for two years. If my ex-husband was still listed as a beneficiary, this could have been a financial disaster. I had also neglected to remove his from some accounts at certain financial institutions. You know those accounts you never touch, like out of sight, out of mind. Pay attention to the names on your accounts. Make sure all of your information is accurate. I had an issue with a credit card when I divorced where the address was changed. I never knew anything about it until I was declined credit because of an unpaid charge. I contacted the credit card company and filed a complaint for unauthorized change of address. I requested the credit card company remove the negative reporting from my credit reports. They complied and my credit score went back up. Of course I was physically and mentally sick over this until it got resolved. What have you neglected? I encourage you to get your arms around anything related to money, including credit.

As a Financial Coach, I offer Financial Wellness by educating families, couples, single individuals, and single parents on how to protect their household income from life events, how to eliminate and reduce debt, and how to set up for retirement. I am happy to share my business with anyone who is looking to start a business or is open to financial education for protecting family and household income. I have found that some people lack basic education on the role of a Financial Coach. We are not door-to-door salespeople. We are here to help you prepare for life changing events, planned and unplanned. It's sad to say, but I declined to talk with a Financial Coach while I was employed. I always felt that I was covered and well taken care of with company benefits: life insurance, health insurance, and my 401(k) contributions. I could not see the forest for the trees. I hear the words of "I'm covered at work" often when I speak to employees about setting up another layer of financial security. What is not being considered is what happens to all the "coverage" once you are no longer an employee. I can tell you firsthand, it disappears. You are left with nothing. That's when the financial sickness can kick in. If you are not careful, you can go into a state of depression. Fight it. Retain your power. It's never too late to recover and bounce back. I did. You can, too.

Your Financial Wellness includes a financial game plan that ensures that YOU and your most valuable human assets are secure. It's as easy as ABC to retain your power. Be proactive. Your life change is one event away. Be prepared. Prepare for possibilities. I am available as a Licensed Financial Coach to assist anyone in need of gaining and retaining their Financial Wellness Power.

SABRINA PROTIC

Sabrina Protic is an energetic and vibrant wife, mother, and grand-mother. She loves educating and empowering her community as a Licensed World-Class Financial Coach, Certified life coach, Author of the Book: *Growing Ageless, Think Young-Live Younger*, collaborative author of *Top 25 Change Makers* and International Streaming Live Co-Host of Thriving Women Talk Network.

Sabrina is the founder of W.E.E. Women's Entrepreneurial, an organization striving for continuous opportunities for women to expand their networks, develop relationships, and grow their businesses. Sabrina is the co-founder of The Sharper Woman Newsletter that is a resource to help women live longer, younger, stronger, and smarter lives utilizing the power of information.

You can connect with Sabrina here: https://www.sabrinaprotic.com.

CHAPTER TWENTY-SEVEN

HEALTH: PUT YOUR HEART INTO IT!

by Scott Leopold
Award Winning Runner, Exercise
Enthusiast, Grandpa
https://facebook.com/scott.leopold1

"I am not a runner like you."
Guess what? I haven't always been a runner either. It's been a journey over many years.

The idea that doing regular cardiovascular activity is critical to heart health is a universally accepted truth. Cardiovascular activity's mental and emotional benefits are well documented as are the heart benefits. Cardiovascular activity is a key to overall wellness. I am an advocate of doing exercise that raises and sustains an elevated heart rate for at least 30 minutes straight at least every other day. Running is my choice of exercise today. I don't run every day; four or five days a week are fine for my body. I do other exercises; some, like cycling and cross-country skiing, provide the sustained elevated heart rate that provides cardiovascular benefit. Other exercises that I do, like weight training and yoga, are done to aid my running by strengthening muscles or increasing flexibility.

As I mentioned, I wasn't always a runner. First, I had to learn how. The focus and discipline necessary to carry out this regimen was not something that came easily to me. In fact, focus and discipline have been an intense, ongoing struggle as long as I can remember. Because of a brain injury that I sustained at birth, my childhood was littered with tests and cognitive screenings to determine the degree to which I would be able to function. Seeds of doubt were sown into my psyche as I was found to have attention deficit issues bordering on hyperactivity, and very slow reactions to both physical and mental challenges. I was "good" at only a few things, and I was below average at a number of things, including coordination and emotional development. However, this was the 1960s, and treatments were few, while the stigma of having a child who was "different" was great. The solution that I was burdened with was to "grow up," since there was a "good chance" that I would grow out of these disturbing behaviors and physical issues.

So there I was, a gangly kid with glasses that had "coke bottle lenses," exceptional in some school subjects, but a miserable wreck in gym class and on the playground. In that era, I may have had a somewhat better school socialization experience if I had been a girl, but since I was a boy, I was often teased and harassed, and I withdrew from others because of it. The only physical activity that I enjoyed was riding my bike. I rode by myself, and by the age of eight, I didn't ask permission to go where I went. I was quite good with maps, and learned where the major roads were relative to my house. I never really got lost, but if my parents knew where I had ridden to, I would have been grounded. However, those rides were some of the rare moments that I felt free and happy.

My struggle with focus, discipline, and self-image continued through secondary schooling, college, and into my career. The subjects that I was good at were never enough to make up for the ones that I fought to learn. I felt as though I was working twice as hard as anyone else to keep up. The same could be said for sports that I enjoyed doing, at least in practice mode. Whether it was basketball, soccer, tennis, track, or football, I felt like endless practice only got me to mediocrity when I played against others. Why couldn't I be good at even one sport? However, I was introduced to cross country skiing by my father at the age of 15, and like the bicycle of my younger days, I enjoyed the solitude of heading down a trail by myself, going wherever I felt inclined to go. If I fell, or looked ungraceful as I saved myself from a fall, those temporary failures didn't matter. I wasn't being timed or graded, I was doing it for my own well-being. I was doing something physical, a sport, and I was enjoying it!

Adulthood and fatherhood brought their own challenges to my life. We had three active children, and I wanted to make sure that they had plenty of opportunities at home to develop intellectually and physically. It took me until I was forty years old to fully realize that I had become unhealthy. I was eating a lot of junk. I ate when I socialized, I ate when I was stressed, I ate when I was bored. Between family and work, I was exhausted. My weight was creeping up into the 220-pound range (I am short of 5 feet 11 inches, and fairly small framed), and I didn't have any activity that allowed me to release stress.

When I was 42 years old, I used a radical diet plan in desperation and managed to get my weight down to around 185 pounds. Around that time, I started hearing from a friend at work that he was running races. He told me what he was doing to train, and about the strategies he was employing during a race. I was intrigued. I had not been a runner for over 25 years (and was never fast), but I felt like it was time to do something that would take me further away from the overweight, sedentary person I had been less than a year before. On an evening at the start of August, I went to a local school track and ran three laps without stopping. I really enjoyed that small accomplishment! I came back to the track two days later and ran five laps without stopping, though I struggled to finish those laps. However, I told my running friend that I had done these small runs. His response was to tell me that there was a two-mile race coming up, it was part of the kickoff to the Illinois State Fair, and hundreds of people would be running it. I told myself that if I could run two miles without stopping before the race date, I would sign up. Two days before the race, I met my goal, and the night before the race, I went to the in-person sign up, filled out the form, and wrote a check. I ran that race, in blue jeans cut-offs that were now too big, with a wallet and a large set of keys in my pockets (what do you do with those things, anyway?). I finished the race in under 17 minutes, and I was pretty excited!

I ran two more races that fall. I started looking at races for the next year, then realized that I would have to develop a regimen to build my endurance, stamina, and speed. Following a regimen meant that I would have to be disciplined. Being disciplined meant that I would have to sharpen my focus and heighten my determination. I had to convince myself that the work necessary was worth it. I started by making a list of the benefits of running in a competitive manner. I needed reasons to be obsessed about running! I came up with these reasons: 1) it was a way to burn more calories and subsequently lose more weight, 2) my cardiovascular system would improve, 3) running was great stress relief, 4) there was a large and active running club in my city, which would enhance my social life, and 5) I had found a challenging sport in which I could perform well. I could see myself developing into a runner who was fast enough to get an occasional award. All these benefits were enough incentive to drive an obsession!

Why do I need an obsession? Because an obsession takes priority over procrastination. An obsession outlasts a resolution. An obsession gets me to put on my running shoes and head out the door without allowing second thoughts or excuses to creep in.

This obsession has made it easy to keep my weight in the range of 150-160 pounds. It has developed my cardiovascular system to the point of being able to run a marathon and have a resting heart rate around 50 beats per minute. It has given me a sense of accomplishment;

for example, I have run just four marathons, but I ran a Boston Marathon qualifying time in three of them, and I have been accepted into the field to run the Boston Marathon again in April of 2022!

This obsession has introduced me to a lot of wonderful people, who I cheer on at races, and who return the favor when they see me racing. It has driven me out the door during stressful times associated with work and a pandemic.

An obsession is often cast in a bad light, because people associate obsession with single-mindedness. We view people who are obsessed as having blinders on that prevent any of the rest of the world from getting in. I propose other synonyms for obsession; fierce determination, laser focus, ultra-motivated. With heart disease still being a number one killer, and an ongoing epidemic of mental health issues including addiction and suicide, it is imperative that we take care of our bodies like they are temples. You wouldn't want to desecrate a temple, or even let it deteriorate from failing to maintain it, yet we seem to make excuses when it comes to even the simple maintenance of our health. Think about the things (or people) you care about the most, and what you would do to protect them, to keep harm away from them so they stay as unsullied as possible. Now apply that passion to your heart health!

Why do I choose the word obsessive? Because I have had it applied to me and my running. "Do you have to run this much?" "You run too much!" "Why are you running today, you ran yesterday?!" "This obsession of yours is extreme!" I hated the criticism, and hated the word obsession at first. In time, though, I realized that what some saw as an obsession had helped me from middle-aged deterioration to golden years vigor and ambition. Yet my "obsession" has not prevented me from being a good husband, father, grandfather, or friend. I have received favorable reviews about all those roles in my life!

If you want to be healthy and embrace wellness, don't embrace half-hearted effort! If only half your heart works, you are not healthy!

We are becoming a society of excuses, where half-heartedness is not just a habit, it's a norm. Intent is a first step, but with heart health and wellness, intent is not sufficient. It is far too easy to fill our lives with other distractions that lead to excuses and inaction. Commit to a specific plan, put it in writing, make copies of the plan, then hang them up all over your work, home, car, or wherever you spend time during your day. Put boxes next to the action items in your plan so you can check them off. Write "Do NOT be half-hearted!" on your plan, and on sticky notes that you post in places where you will see them frequently.

A half-hearted effort will lead to failure and frustration in any endeavor. Don't fall back into the half-hearted habit when it comes to the health of your heart.

Be obsessive about your heart for the "well" of it!

SCOTT LEOPOLD

Scott Leopold is an award-winning runner, meteorologist and grand-pa. He has successfully run 900-1,800 miles per year for the last 18 years. In severe weather, he can often be found storm chasing. After working in air pollution regulation for 31 years, he retired in 2020. Scott has qualified for the Boston Marathon three times and will run in 2022 as a 60-year-old. As a first-time author, he hopes to inspire people to understand it's never too late to improve your health.

You can connect with Scott here:

https://facebook.com/scott.leopold1.

CHAPTER TWENTY-EIGHT

DIMENSIONS OF WELLNESS GUIDE ME TO OPTIMUM HEALTH

by Shanna Lee Moore
Owner, Justice Massage & Developing
True Health
www.developingtruehealth.com

Wellness is defined as "the quality or state of being in good health especially as an actively sought goal." In my life there have been ebbs and flows to this journey. At each new turn or season of my life I'm presented with new information. It has been said that "knowledge is power;" however, it is only potential power unless it's applied. What I once believed to be acceptable practices are no longer in alignment with my highest self. As I continue to grow into the best version of myself, I get opportunities to create wellness in more areas of my life.

I became a certified massage therapist in 2007. I believe that was just the start of my wellness journey. I got to learn about the physical body and how it functions. Also that the different systems and organs had different responsibilities. Massage has many health benefits for the physical body and also some that carry over into the mental health realm.

Even though I was helping to facilitate health in others, my own body wasn't performing at its optimal level. I hadn't taken the best care of myself and previous circumstances had allowed unhealthy habits to develop. I was overweight and taking several prescription medications on a daily basis. I had put trust in doctors and Western medicine and just listened to the diagnoses without questioning anything or doing my due diligence. I didn't even think I was that unhealthy.

I am so glad I was able to change my water and change my life! When I started drinking electrolyzed reduced water my body responded positively. Since the body is 75% water it makes sense that getting the correct type of water in it will make an impact quicker than other methods might. I was praised for the results I achieved; however, since I didn't "work" for them with diet or exercise I felt bad taking credit. I just wanted everyone to experience the benefits of being properly hydrated. This also started me on the financial wellness track since I learned about different ways to create income. You don't know what you don't know, so I'm grateful that someone took the time to reach out to me and give me new ideas to implement.

The next thing I learned about was reading labels on food, nutrition from Whole Food sources, and all the pollutants and chemicals that are in our diet. Now, I am by no means perfect when it comes to this. I like to practice the 80/20 rule. As long as I'm choosing whole, nutrient rich food 80% of the time, then I feel like the other 20% can be spent more freely. Sometimes you just want that cheesecake! My body has started communicating more after I eat certain foods and as I get better at listening I can make more refined choices. I always want to feel my best and that requires checking in with my body and on a vibrational level to see what is no longer serving me. It makes me sad that so many of us just learn to live in pain. Greater awareness of my body and how it reacts allows me the opportunity to make better choices for myself in the future.

In addition to what I put IN my body I also need to be mindful of what influences my mind. Stinkin' thinkin' doesn't do anybody any good. Our minds are our most powerful resource. Anything we think about we can create and achieve. So much of my life was spent without this awareness. Now I know the importance of guarding my thoughts. By making sure that I read good books, associate with quality people, listen to productive podcasts or audios, and play positive music I can increase my mental wellness. I so wish this information was taught to me as a child. My prayer is that as I learn the skills and techniques to prosper, I can teach them to my children and others so that they may longer benefit from the knowledge. Breaking established paradigms is much harder than just learning something the first time. I have been working on my mindset and will continue to feed the optimistic and positive side more than the pessimistic, doubtful one. It is a daily decision to seek truth and apply it by taking ACTION.

Getting into gratitude and remembering my mission to serve others helps. I am no good to anyone else if my cup is empty or full of toxic substances. Getting into community with those who seek truth and share in love was the next phase of growth that I took. I never wanted to cut ties or give up on others from my past; however, there came to be a point where I realized I can't drag them along with me either. We are all given free will and it is up to us what choices we make. My gifts and talents will help more people when I focus on those who are open minded and hungry for change.

As I learned about myself at a holistic level, I started to see how everything is connected. While preparing this chapter I found an article that stated there are 7 dimensions of wellness. These are Physical, Emotional, Intellectual, Social, Spiritual, Environmental, and Occupational. I feel that as I journey deeper into knowing myself more is revealed within these categories. I will share some of the most helpful tools I've learned along the way. As a disclaimer, no two people are the same, so one must always tune in to their own body and see what techniques work best.

The Physical Dimension was addressed with my body's return to homeostasis. After the chemicals were detoxed from my body and I started being more mindful of the fuel I consumed, I was then able to add in movement and exercise. I like having fun so most of my workouts include recreational activities such as skating, dancing, and walking with my dog or friends. I have taken Qi Gong training as well and love how it incorporates breath and movement. Taking a deep breath in is actually linked to the sympathetic nervous system, which controls the fight-or-flight response. Exhaling is linked to the parasympathetic nervous system, which influences our body's ability to relax and calm down. This can also aid our emotional wellness.

My Emotional wellness flourished with my ability to accept my past experiences and use them to grow instead of letting them dictate my future. Finding forgiveness for myself and others and getting support to release what was once holding me back. I also found affirmations to be helpful for my emotional health, as well as guided meditations before bed to influence the subconscious mind.

Intellectual wellness is addressed and strengthened with my desire to learn and grow daily. All of the new knowledge internalized and put into practice. Continuing to glean from those who have achieved what I consider successful results. Also stepping into my uniqueness. That leads into the Social dimension.

Only when I fully embrace myself for who I am and what I can offer can I truly contribute. I know we all have special qualities and when we combine them we can achieve Greatness. We are designed to live within communities so that where one is weak another's strength can come in and provide balance.

This school of thought has allowed me to find Spiritual wellness. I cultivate a relationship with my creator and use my faith to seek out my purpose for being here. This attracts others to me so we can journey together and lift each other up. True joy can be experienced in all phases of life. It is not the same as the world's version of happiness which is circumstantial.

My Environmental wellness improved as I cleared my mind and wanted to also clear space in my surroundings. Deleting unneeded emails and throwing away junk mail or old paperwork. Giving away clothes that no longer sparked joy for me or could bring happiness to others. Also getting out into nature and reconnecting with Mother Earth. I've become more sensitive to overstimulation and need to step back at times to regroup.

The last dimension of wellness is Occupational. This is where I get to use all my new realizations and create the life I've always wanted. The combination of nurturing all the areas of wellness to develop true health, along with continuing to search for knowledge in areas that were taught incorrectly or never questioned is what my journey has been all about.

I am now using my voice (and pen) to speak up against injustices. To offer hope to those who feel something is "off" but can't put their finger on it. To restore balance through proper education and implementation of systems to help the "little" guys and gals. To bring harmony in my internal world and let it flow over into the lives of all I come into contact with.

It took me a long time to see my worth, to know I was valuable, and that I had a purpose for living. To fully understand that the power to change my circumstances was within ME. That just because something was spoken to me, didn't mean I had to accept it, internalize and let it define me. This book is "Wellness for Winners" and some days I still don't feel like I've arrived or "won." This life is an experience and each day is a new chance to live it to the fullest. I get a new sunrise to shine light on my path and a beautiful sunset that paints the sky like a canvas. I can ask "What else is Possible?" and discover ways to acquire my greatest dreams and desires. I get to stand in my power as a woman, wife, mother, sister, daughter, and friend to those in my circle. Every day is another chance to know I am created in the image of the Most High and that His plan for my life is abundance and love.

One of my passions is sharing what I've learned along the way so that others can get what they long for. Nothing is more rewarding than to be able to teach different perspectives and watch them grow. To see the light bulb go off in their eyes when they really get it.

Another gift of mine is writing poetry, so I always like to include one in my story.

One of my gifts is writing, you see.
It is the one way I can communicate clearly.

There's no chance to stumble or stutter over my words.
It gives my ideas a chance to flow out and it's how I feel most heard.

I am so grateful for books and poetic expression.
The blessings of writing to get over my depression.

Lyrics in songs and music to dance to. What things mean the most to you?

Spend time discovering all your passions and gifts.
Take quiet time and write yourself a list.

Try to do something each day you enjoy. Life doesn't have to be so serious, you can still play with toys.

I still have a collection of those to admire.
Remembering childhood fun should never be retired.

Wellness is balance and harmony in life.
Release the stress and give up the strife.

Find your community, tribe or family to love.
And if you're still searching you can look up above.

You were loved and supported before this earthly place.
I hope hearing that puts a smile on your face.

Passion and purpose are like a fire burning bright.
Let them out so you can shine your light!

So if I could leave you with just one takeaway it would be: Do You Boo Boo! Don't let self-doubt, worry, imposter syndrome, or others' judgments of you stop you from reaching your full potential. You are a star, so go out there and SHINE!

SHANNA LEE MOORE

Shanna Lee Moore is an entrepreneur and international #1 best-selling author. Her passion is helping others create the life they've always wanted. Shanna offers creative solutions and out-of-the-box thinking to help people balance their families and businesses.

You can connect with Shanna Lee here:
www.developingtruehealth.com.

CHAPTER TWENTY-NINE

NO, I'M NOT CRAZY....

by Tamara Carruthers
Owner, The Messy Canvas
https://instagram.com/messy_canvas_tc

Somehow the admission to people that I was suffering from a mental disorder made them think I was crazy... not because I was suffering, but because I was telling them that I was suffering and THAT made me crazy.

Mental illness is something very real to me. I have a long family history of mental disorders. I have members suffering on a daily basis at this very moment and some that have passed away. And I often wonder if they had felt comfortable enough to say they were suffering would their lives turn out differently. All I know is that I didn't want to take any chance! As much as I love them, I didn't want my life to turn out like theirs.

For me, my mental disorder has been diagnosed as severe anxiety, depression, and post-traumatic stress disorder.

In 2016, at the age of 36, I was diagnosed with stage 3 colon cancer. I was a fairly healthy person: I did yoga, I tried to eat right and drank plenty of water, you know all the things "healthy" people do. So how did this happen to me! My first thought was what did I do to deserve this!

I am often asked how I knew something was wrong. I had numerous symptoms before my diagnosis. Did you ignore the signs? Actually, no! I visited the doctor every time I had a "stomach issue." I was diagnosed with IBS, hemorrhoids, ulcers, and one point was told it was just stress!

All this leading up to the day that I was so tired and fatigued that I could barely walk. I visited a doctor that day! I explained to the doctor my symptoms, which included throwing up that morning, blood in my stool a week before, and the extreme fatigue. He immediately sent me to see a GI doctor, who immediately scheduled a colonoscopy.

The day of the colonoscopy seemed pretty normal. I was scheduled for an upper and lower GI.

Before I could fully wake up from the anesthesia, the nurse was shaking me awake and advised me that I needed to head straight over to get a CT scan because the doctor had spotted a growth on my colon!

This was Day 1 of my anxiety attacks that would become debilitating. I had suffered from depression before as well as anxiety, but nothing could come close to the feeling I was having at that moment. Because I knew that a growth in my colon could be the big C word!

The doctor had taken a biopsy which he sent to be tested, so I had to wait five days before I would know what was to become of my life. Each day a PEACE of my soul was leaving me. I had no clue what to expect and at the same time I had killed myself and resurrected at least 3-4 times Googling my symptoms!

Every day the anxiety was building up. Anxiety wasn't new to me. Over the years I would feel anxiety build up inside of me and then push it aside mainly because I didn't know what to do with those emotions. I just couldn't identify what I was dealing with, and I had no one to discuss it with.

Acknowledging or even discussing mental illness in my family just NEVER happened. I have family members who were diagnosed with mental illness, yet they were hidden away and we never saw them. And on the slight chance that we did witness any "abnormal behavior," they would have them removed immediately.

So for YEARS I hid it. I have experienced many episodes over the years. All while going through a horribly abusive relationship, which I also hid. The truth of the matter was I was mentally tormented and weak, and I stayed in that abuse for two years because I was afraid to tell the truth. The anxiety of telling the truth to me was far worse than the beatings. The embarrassment and the shame were all too consuming.

In 2014 I started to have episodes where all I could do was cry out to my best friend and my mother. Literally called crying, screaming, and yelling. I was no longer in control of my emotions. I couldn't hide them; I was a mess.

Yet, I left a physically abusive relationship and head on over to a mentally abusive relationship.

In this relationship for two years, I dealt with a lot of emotional abuse that was causing me to literally be sick. Sick to my stomach, mentally unstable, and my spirit was just broken.

In 2016 my life changed forever! Two days before I was to have surgery to have cancer removed from my body, the surgeon told me due to the location of my tumor there was a possibility that I would have to receive a colostomy bag after surgery. I was completely devastated just at the thought.

I was a nervous wreck. But right before I was supposed to go into surgery my aunt prayed over me and asked God to cover and heal me. I went into the surgery with complete peace of mind. Confident that they would get all the cancer out. I would only be at a stage one or two which meant we caught it early enough and I wouldn't need any further treatment. I was prepared to recover and get back to my normal life.

I recovered quickly from surgery. I had a couple of setbacks, but nothing major. On my fourth day in the hospital, I was ready to be released. Every day I had asked the doctor for the results of the pathology report. And finally on day four we received them.

I had done my research, so I was familiar with some of the terminology he was using so the moment I heard that the tumor had penetrated my colon wall and attached to my lymph node I knew that my life was about to completely change. This meant that I was now at stage 3 and chemotherapy would be necessary to increase my chances of survival.

At that moment, all the blood in my body rushed to my feet. I was numb. I was sweating, but I was freezing cold. My feet wouldn't move and no words would come out of my mouth. My chest was burning. It felt like no air was circulating. It was the mother lode of panic attacks.

And then I went silent. But my mind was racing. I needed answers, but I didn't want the wrong answer so I sat there inside my head! My kids were there and aware of what was going on, but not really understanding that mommy could die. And that hurt more than anything!

One day, while I was at my pity party, my daughters were playing and laughing trying to make me laugh. I tried! I remember that day vividly because I cried so much after they went to sleep that my face and eyeballs burned. And then a voice (who I pray was God) said "it's your time"!

I really started freaking out, "God, NO, not yet! I want see my babies become mothers and a father I want great grandkids!" The next morning I was afraid to open my eyes because I thought that I'd be enclosed in a box with ugly funeral makeup on and some jacked up hairstyle. I could hear my children close by, the baby girl whining. So my motherly instinct that had somehow been removed the last few days immediately kicked in and I hopped up to comfort my baby.

I hopped up out of bed and not a casket! I was alive. And my baby girl wasn't really whining; they were playing with their baby dolls. I was alive! In my bed and not in a casket with ugly makeup and jacked up hair!

That day began my fight! God wasn't ready for me yet. And that message "it's your time" meant my time to live and fight. So for six months of chemotherapy, I fought! It was hard, painful, and scary, but I fought! And after six months I was cancer free!

Nothing about your life is regular after cancer! My body had endured six months of poison being shot through my veins. My body would never be the same. I now have allergies, asthma, and sinus issues. I had neuropathy in my hands and feet, which made simple things like walking and writing a task.

While surviving all of those things, my anxiety was at an all-time high. Debilitating even.

One morning I finally got up the courage to say, "Hey, I'm not ok." I had spent days just to myself. I was driving to work during a panic attack one morning. So as I pulled into the parking garage, I cried as hard as I could before I had to put on my "normal face." But this particular day there was no way. I could feel my hands starting to sweat, my heart started racing, my mind tried to process the fact that yup you are about to breakdown right here right now! I made it to the basement bathroom before anyone could see me and I cried until my head hurt.

Over a period of three weeks I had these same episodes several times. Finally, I needed to go see a psychiatrist, not just a therapist, but I needed to be medicated!

Immediately after that session I was more drained than I had been before going. I was ready to start taking the medication that the doctor prescribed and get back in balance. It just didn't happen.

That day ended with me jumping out of a moving car, attempting to walk home on a busy street, and then finally to the hospital, where I was given medication for my severe anxiety.

A lot of African-American women that I know just don't want to seek therapy. We are the backbone of the family. We are supposed to be strong and keep it together no matter what. We have been taught that we have to be STRONG! But it's ok to not be ok!

My first PEACE of advice, forget what people say! Good, bad, or indifferent. Find strength and peace in knowing yourself and your limits, and act accordingly. Find trusted supporters.

Tell your supporters your triggers and let them know what helps you cope when you have an episode. The goal is to still be able to enjoy life, but at your limits. Don't let people push you beyond your limits. Take baby steps to become more comfortable in uncomfortable situations. You and only you should push your limits.

My safe place is "The Quad." They are a group of trusted friends. They know what they need to know about me and my mental health. Twice a year we participate in a mental cleanse. We share how it helped and methods we have used.

Seek professional help. Therapists/psychiatrists are trained to understand the human mind and emotions. With that said, every therapist/psychiatrist is not for everyone. Find someone you are comfortable with. Be honest with your provider. It allows them to focus on the methods that will benefit you. Set appointments and keep them. Make sure it's at a time of day where you have the least distractions. Not only that, make sure you have time and space afterwards to process what you have learned or shared about yourself. It takes a lot of you to be completely transparent.

Finally, meditate and pray. The benefits of mediation are both mental and physical. Take time with yourself. Take time with God!

Though my anxiety disorder is an everyday struggle, I now realize that I have the power to control the outcome. I may need assistance from a friend, professional, or even medication, but I am ahead of it and taking it with stride each day.

TAMARA CARRUTHERS

Tamara Carruthers is a wife, mother, sister, daughter, friend and self-lover with an entrepreneurial heart and creative spirit. Tamara's joy in life is being a servant leader while spreading love and peace to everyone she encounters.

Connect with Tamara here https://instagram.com/messy_canvas_tc.

CHAPTER THIRTY

MOMMIN IT LIKE A BOSS IS A LIFESTYLE WITH PURPOSE AND GRACE

by Whitney Gonzalez-Hartford
CEO, Mommin It Like A Boss
www.momminitlikeaboss.com

Parenthood is hard. It's not always easy to parent with a graceful heart; however, I'm excited to share that through the last five years, my journey as a single mother facing infertility has led me to where I am now: a happily married mother of three beautiful girls finding comfort in my chaos.

Now, let's get one thing straight. I don't have all the answers to this parenting thing. I've learned some tricks through my own life experiences and through the guidance of others which has helped prepare me, but there are many things I have shown up so unprepared for, one of these being postpartum recovery. I wish my amazing ObGyn would have shared more of her knowledge on this leg of pregnancy and motherhood. I was considered high-risk throughout my pregnancy and, although she inspired me to stay active during my pregnancy, there are many things I had to learn on my own. Nevertheless, I forged my own path figuring out a postpartum journey that worked for my body! Now, I am able to share a comprehensive postpartum roadmap with others which helps them to conquer the fourth trimester that often goes neglected. These tips and tricks I wish I would have known can help all mothers in some way find comfort in their chaos and inspiration to Mommin It Like A Boss!

Let's take it back to the beginning. Growing up, I had this vision of what life would be like as a first-time mom (as I'm sure it's something most little girls dream of). As the future came into fruition, it turned out to be the opposite. Being a young mother at 22, I had to take on life day by day, solely focusing on surviving motherhood and providing for my daughter. Being a provider and mother didn't leave me any time to focus on myself, and after a challenging pregnancy, I didn't enter motherhood understanding the value of self-care and how it would benefit not only myself, but those around me.

Postpartum recovery was challenging after my first daughter, Nalah, was born. Life swept me up and before I knew it, I found myself irregularly exercising while consuming fast food. Since I was young, I didn't think those habits would catch up with me. As an adult, I had to make a change. The overwhelming, ever consuming, feeling of burnout and loss of purpose contributed greatly to my daily choices. I'm positive every mother has experienced this during some part of motherhood, running on a never-ending hamster wheel putting out one fire just to turn around to another one. Those emotions and day-to-day struggle was something I felt for about three years, when I stopped wishing for change and made it.

Changing my lifestyle was a must. I wanted better for me and my daughter. It's not easy to work through depression, anxiety, and stress while also balancing work and Mommin It Like A Boss. Even though I knew some steps to take that would help navigate those emotions, it was hard to start. I knew working out always brought me clarity and helped me to feel better and, while I didn't necessarily want to work out, I craved the feeling of success and accomplishment I felt after I completed one. So, that's what I did. I started to feel comfortable saying, "no," to distractions. I focused on my little family's happiness and how I could achieve more happiness only being a family of two. My daughter and I started working out in fun ways together, sharing chocolate protein shakes, and spending quality time together. Nalah and I loved it.

Have you ever wanted to workout and get into shape, but then wonder how on earth you would balance that while you had children to care for at the same time? Are you feeling so tired after work or wondering when, in the small amounts of time you do have, when you would fit in a workout? Those were the discouraging thoughts I felt for the longest time that kept me from making change. When I realized it was my mindset holding me back and not these imaginary obstacles, I stopped letting those negative thoughts stop me from achieving my goals. I started peer fitting, spinning, boxing, and doing whatever fitness activities felt right for my body. Nalah and I even did a 5k glow color run together when she was five years old! I was able to get our little family of two on track and it was such a relief.

Another several years into my journey, I met my best friend and the love of my life. He completed our family and we had a beautiful wedding. I had prayed for a good father for Nalah and when he walked into our lives, everything felt right. This didn't come without its own struggles and hardships. We faced our own complications years down the road, but having a solid foundation and Mommin It Like A Boss lifestyle is what helped me get through a trying and humbling time with a purpose. The season of life we were struggling with delivered us daunting news, that In Vitro Fertilization (IVF) was the only option we could choose if we wanted to grow our family. It was devastating news for us and we felt as though our hearts had shattered. Never in a million years did I think we would experience infertility. Through this news, self-care is what saved my sanity.

Through prayer, patience, self-care, exercise and two rounds of IVF, we were successful. I'm thankful for the mindset change I had established years earlier, because maintaining an active lifestyle had helped me to work through positive and negative seasons. In short, my IVF experience kept me busy. I had three to six one-hour long drives to our IVF doctor for all my appointments. It probably goes without saying, but through IVF, we experienced a rollercoaster of emotions, from disappointment to embarrassment. This, of course, was exacerbated through the 50 or so hormone shots I had to take over the course of three months. In moments of helplessness, having a consistent self-care routine, exercise schedule, and channeling my spirituality was key to getting through this experience. At the end of it all, we were blessed to have a successful round of IVF giving us not only one, but two babies!

I found out I was pregnant with twins the day before I turned 30. That news was a blessing and the best birthday gift I could ask for. Through the good news, we also came to terms with the reality of IVF and the shots continued. For the first ten weeks of my pregnancy, I had to continue taking my hormone shots just to sustain it. I had to balance morning sickness with the shots which left me counting down the weeks and playing mind games with myself to work through the pain. Although we were incredibly happy, we were also nervous and it didn't help that we were constantly reminded that we had a high-risk pregnancy. This made me feel disabled, as there were so many things I was unable to do.

I learned through all of these experiences the importance of keeping the company of those who inspire me. I have been inspired by different people throughout my life, but one that sticks out is my ObGyn. She encouraged me to continue on with my manageable Mommin It Like A Boss lifestyle throughout my pregnancy with my twins. I was thankful for this advice because I knew how imperative it would be for my mental health to continue on with my healthy lifestyle through self-care during pregnancy and postpartum, whether this was working out or taking a relaxing bath.

Overall, my pregnancy with my twins was healthier than my first. I promised to myself after all we had gone through, I would have to take Mommin It Like A Boss to a whole new level after having the twins! I was in denial about getting a C-section, yet prepared myself because it was a great possibility. I continued to work until I went on maternity leave and it was a week later that the twins were here via C-section. I think we all can agree giving birth or having surgery are the least glamorous parts of pregnancy and the most painful.

With twins in the NICU a day after my C-section, I was Mommin It Like A Boss up the halls with my breast pump every two hours to pump while I was visiting my babies in the NICU. I felt like life was getting sucked out of me because I was breastfeeding and pumping for several hours a day! Not only had I just given birth, but my body was in overdrive trying to produce milk for the girls. The following day, I was walking with the help of a walker to see my girls in the NICU. Luckily, we were only in the NICU for thirteen days and took our tiny, 4lb baby girls home. While we were happy to have them home, we weren't ready! We had the support of our families to help us through this transition period and they graced us with meal preparations, nighttime feeding assistance, and house cleaners.

With the support they provided during their visits, my husband and I were able to take time to recharge and take care of ourselves as well. Postpartum self-care might be the most important time to exercise! Your bodies need all of the rest and nutrition it can take and taking time during postpartum recovery is crucial. When our babies are born, we forget to take care of ourselves while we take care of the baby. Our bodies are experiencing hormonal changes and stressors every single day. Mommin It Like A Boss is a lifestyle and choice we make every day starting the moment our blessings come into our lives. Postpartum recovery is not about judging yourself the moment you've given birth, it's knowing you have options after having children. Just because life changes, doesn't mean it's a journey you have to do alone. You don't have to hold onto the baby weight when your children aren't babies anymore. There are amazing postpartum options available to you!

Mommin It Like A Boss is my goal most days, but I have learned to find comfort in my chaos and the healthier I am the happier I feel. The lifestyle workout regimens I do are manageable, family-friendly, and focus on postpartum recovery health and wellness. It's a journey that takes mental and physical commitment. Keeping active has helped me mentally work through the hormones as my body has transitioned through postpartum. My oldest is now ten, the twins are now toddlers, and I have maintained my active lifestyle and I'm a happy, thriving mompreneur and CEO of Bangin Vintage! I wouldn't have made it this far without Mommin It Like A Boss, the support of my family and friends who have inspired and encouraged me!

If you find it challenging to lose the baby weight or get into a rhythm that's less stressful with your new blessing or blessings, I strongly encourage a mentor or motivational coach. Moms want to enjoy our children while looking and feeling our best. This is possible to achieve with some guidance, commitment, and patience! This is what I specialize in, and I can't wait to assist new and veteran moms get their health and confidence back. Contact me at www.momminitlikeaboss.com or improveyourlifelv@gmail.com to work out your postpartum body and into your new you!

WHITNEY GONZALEZ-HARTFORD

Moms face many physical and mental challenges during pregnancy and postpartum recovery. In 2019, Whitney Gonzalez-Hartford's life changed and she became a twin mom/mother of three. Whitney's life became more chaotic and she started Mommin It Like A Boss because with three kids that's what moms do. She used her experiences to motivate and educate expecting/new mothers by offering online workshops and programs that provide them with the tools to take care of their health/wellness as they transition into motherhood, which can be an exhausting and rewarding experience.

Whitney's Mission is to educate, inspire, and empower expecting/new mothers through their pregnancy journey into postpartum by offering them encouragement and healthier lifestyle choices that will make their recovery process so much smoother.

Connect with Whitney here: www.MomminItLikeABoss.com.

AFTERWORD

It is our sincere hope that these stories have not only caused you to think, but to ACT! As you have read through the chapters, you have seen the authors experience many challenges. You probably also noticed they made a decision to uplevel their life. Some stories highlighted mental or emotional health or wellness, and some physical or spiritual wellness and, yet others, financial wellness. The common thread through all of our stories is that we chose not to stay stuck in a state of unwellness or unhappiness.

May today be the day you are inspired to choose to create the life you deserve, be courageous enough to act, and surround yourself with winners who want you to win as well.

Today is the perfect day to Take Action!

If any of these stories resonated with you, please connect with the author. They are here to help you Win in Wellness.

Sherri Leopold and Evan Trad and our Wellness Winners

CPSIA information can be obtained
at www.ICGtesting.com
Printed in the USA
BVHW071942220222
629775BV00001B/184